Pelican Books
The Grammar of Living

David Cooper was born in Cape Town,
South Africa, in 1931. He graduated from the
University of Cape Town in 1955 and then
came to London, where he held a series of
hospital posts. In the last of these he directed
the experimental unit for young schizophrenics
called Villa 21. His principal concern has been
to develop existential psychiatry in Britain
and to overcome the methodological difficulties
and compartmentalization of the human
sciences. He is a founder member of the
Philadelphia Association, London, and was
Director of the Institute of Phenomenological
Studies. Among his works are *Reason and
Madness* (with R. D. Laing), *Psychiatry and
Anti-psychiatry* and *The Death of the Family*.
He edited the Pelican Original, *The Dialectics
of Liberation*.

David Cooper

The Grammar of Living

An Examination of Political Acts

Penguin Books

Penguin Books Ltd,
Harmondsworth, Middlesex, England
Penguin Books Australia Ltd,
Ringwood, Victoria, Australia
Penguin Books Canada Ltd,
41 Steelcase Road West, Markham, Ontario, Canada
Penguin Books (N.Z.) Ltd,
182–190 Wairau Road, Auckland 10, New Zealand

First published by Allen Lane 1974
Published in Pelican Books 1976

Made and printed in Great Britain by
Richard Clay (The Chaucer Press) Ltd, Bungay, Suffolk
Set in Monotype Garamond

To those who will survive and those
who do survive their deaths.

To all the countless anonymous revolutionaries,
mad poets and poetic madmen in the world
who will never submit.

Contents

Introduction

I have decided to write a short book rather than a long one because, although many of the issues I treat could be expanded, I prefer to leave much of the work of expansion to the reader – not out of any sort of maliciousness but out of a due regard for the necessity, given the impetus, to think things out fully in the course of revolutionary work, work both on oneself and on the whole society. Also revolutionary work necessitates brevity. Besides there are far too many books that say in a hundred pages what could more profitably for everyone be said in a paragraph. I sometimes think that Sartre's brief pre-war book *The Transcendence of the Ego* is in many ways more important than the monumental *Being and Nothingness* and the *Critique of Dialectical Reason* or the voluminous studies on Genet and Flaubert.

Before Neil Middleton, who has helped me so much in the publication of my writings, mentioned politics as 'the grammar of living', I was going to call this volume 'The Book of Lies', to be succeeded by 'The Book of Truth'. After discovering that Aleister Crowley had written a *Book of Lies* I decided simply to give it the title 'NO!' Finally, however, I decided to use Neil's phrase: I would never write a book that attempts to *spell* out solutions but only to hint at a *grammar* or possible series of grammars of such a nature that the 'rules' invite the reader to break them with a view to forming progressively liberated structures of experience. Grammars of living are concerned with the modes of structuring of risk in full lucidity in each situation in life. The attitude of not risking is obedience to the alien imperative for nothing more than the suicidal security of one's private convenience. The risk is to assume responsibility when no choices remain.

The material in this volume issues mainly from active workshops I have had with my comrades so that body as well as cerebral work has been involved. Some of the contents were learned in seminar-dialogues, others were learned in the dream and love laboratory of bed – one of the best universities I know. Some were learned during various personal experiences of incarceration.

It may seem ambitious, to say the least, to attempt to eliminate 'the unconscious' and all notions of self while paradoxically having to use 'self language'. On the contrary the *coup d'état* of the self and in particular the unconscious self seems to me to be remarkably obvious at this historical juncture, as does the replacement of 'economic' concepts by non-metric ones. Remarkably obvious because of the determinism and the limitation of political responsibility implied by the usual usage of these former concepts.

We are henceforth fully responsible for our 'unconscious acts' – we have to answer for them to the whole society.

In order to extend psychoanalytic concepts and forms of praxis and ground them phenomenologically rather than see them as narrow mechanisms, I have had to use language in new ways. For example 'life re-lived' subsumes psychoanalytic regression in a broader concept of 'going back'. The technique of interpretation is examined in relation to a different mode of being with the other that I term 'responses' – this has to do with the most basic human need for a witness. I also explore psycho-analytic notions such as the distinction between 'inner' and 'outer' and then introjection and projection by the paradoxical use of language such as heading the relevant segment or chapter 'The Inner is the Outer'. Sometimes, again, a sort of poetry seems to be the most appropriate form of discourse, and so on.

Further, instead of forming regular chapters, I have decided to let the material fall into natural segments. This is not only more natural but allows the reader, more or less, to plunge in at any point. Compared to my last book *The Death of the Family** I have decided on a style that can no longer be critically described as 'brilliant but wildly chaotic', 'preposterous, obscene, crazy' but will merit a rather cooler reception that will accord with a change in my life style since I came back to live in the third world, principally Argentina (I spent the first quarter of a century of my life in South Africa). *The Death of the Family* was largely a revolt against first-world values; now I hope I shall combine bitter attack with a quieter feeling. I must confess that I spent the first twenty-five years of my life in the third world hardly recognizing it and the next sixteen years in the first world (mainly Europe) without remembering what I had hardly recognized. I now aim to destroy alienated language by using it against itself – just as sex was invented to destroy sexual love, so language was invented to destroy communication, which in turn has been used to destroy communion. The strategy must be to use what destroys us to destroy what destroys us so as to liberate quite specific zones of hope.

* David Cooper, *The Death of the Family*, Allen Lane The Penguin Press, 1971; Penguin Books, 1973.

When I came back on a second visit to South America it took me several months to realize I was in the third world and to discover the meaning of the motto 'The Third World first'. My aim was to assist in the formation of anti-psychiatric communes and an international teaching-learning centre in the third world so that Europeans and North Americans would come here not to teach but to learn, thus helping attack cultural imperialism. Argentina is a favourable ground for this slow work firstly because its psychoanalytic tradition (e.g. Pichon-Rivière, Emilio Rodrigué, Marie Langer) breeds rebellion and breakaway groups; secondly because comradeship links are more extensive and lead to easier exitus from the nuclear family than in the first world; thirdly because after North America Argentina is perhaps the most heavily psychiatrized country in the world and lots of psychiatry makes for lots of anti-psychiatry; fourthly the fluid political scene makes for a good, usable, individual fluidity. I mention these matters because so much of the content of this book has been determined by my experiences in Argentina.

In writing of politics and revolution here I am not, as might seem to be the case, widening these concepts beyond all recognized usage, but rather I am trying to give them their full dimensionality. Politics has to do with the deployment of power in or between social entities – here I do introduce an erasable distinction between the human social state (of affairs) and other states (of nature). I do not actually depart from the Greek sense of πολιτεία meaning either the citizenship or the condition of a state. I wish to underline the 'erasable' distinction between the human, social and other states of nature because, although there is a qualitative not merely quantitative difference, all are part of one being and that which is beyond human

4

being, a 'beyond' into which we plunge ourselves by an experiential act of 'erasure', is beyond all of that One Being – hence the death of the 'one and only' God – and the transcending leap into what is beyond the God we have been taught about.

For much of the history of natural science the observer/observed dichotomy has remained absolute. In the most recent physical science it has been recognized with a shocking impact that the observer or the observing equipment is modified by the observing act. In the human sciences the modification of the observer by observing is universal and the *qualitative* difference now emerges that the very instrument of knowing the observed, on the part of the observer, is nothing less than the particular modification of the observer by observing. There is nothing of solipsism of subjectivism in this since the observer can be similarly observed by other observers and a unitary plenum of being of all nature remains. It remains, I believe, to be transcended but before we speak of cosmopolitics (as if *speaking* of it were in any sense relevant) we have to consider 'the Political' in the course of the mundane. All previous mystifications about the political may have been historically intelligible but are now unnecessary. Some new counter-mystifications may be necessary as part of a political therapeia but I shall try strictly to limit those I may introduce.

If *part* of a social entity is changed we speak either of progress (or reform) or reaction. If an attempt is made to change a *whole* social entity we speak of revolution or counter-revolution. In the first chapter I examine what these 'social entities' might be.

Having said this much I wish only to add a general apologia for this book. If I write with either light or heavy irony of the pigs of society, it is because *it is never*

compassionate to show compassion to the enemies of compassion.
An apologia for the disorder of this book is ironic since I
hope that you will find it usefully *disordering* rather than
'just' disorder:

> Lacking a birth in disorder,
> The enlivening detestation of order,
> No liberating discipline can ever see
> or be the light of a new day.

I have tried to write a book for you if you are the person
who thinks you are the person who I also think you are.
In the course of reading whatever you choose to read or
unread or not read between the covers that enclose these
pages I hope we shall break out of the constricting positions of reader versus writer versus reader so that we
arrive at the sense of an invisible, intangible but wholly
non-anonymous relation of loving separateness. I hope to
raise a number of questions that, without perversity, I
have refrained from attempting to answer myself, but I
also hope that the questions that might be raised in your
mind are such that if you listen to the way you ask the
question you might begin to know the answer. Listening
to oneself is always the precondition to hearing the
message of anyone else. As I write I shall try to find a
way of listening to you.

> Wherever you are or I am is here
> Wherever here is
> But wherever here is
> Let us not let it be anywhere else.

I

The Political Act

Imperialists will never become Buddhas until their doom.

Chairman Mao Tse-tung

On se couche dans l'herbe et l'on s'écoute vivre,
De l'odeur du foin vert à loisir on s'enivre,
Et sans penser à rien on regarde les cieux ...
Hélas! une voix crie: 'En voiture, messieurs '!*

Gérard de Nerval

Firstly, and this is most relevant to the title of this chapter, I would like to express my total opposition to the conventional form of writing books. This form, which implies the binary role structure of writer versus reader, is a type of social violence that, through its non-mutuality and non-reciprocity, can lead only to the enslavement of the minds of both the so-called 'writer' and the so-called 'reader'. It is a method of social control, a method of micro-political manipulation of persons, which, in an exploitative society, can lead only to a false mutuality – a mutuality of exploitation that reinforces the system

* From a bed of grass you hear yourself living,
  With the smell of green hay you get drunk at your leisure,
  Thoughtlessly you stare into the sky above ...
  But alas a voice screams out: 'All aboard, gentlemen!'

that oppresses us all. The unidirectional binary role structure represents the same violence in other areas of experience and behaviour, for example therapist/therapeutized, analyst/analysand, torturer/tortured, colonizer/colonized and so on.

In, say, the teacher/taught structure the 'teacher' externalizes her or his capacity to learn into the 'taught' who in turn externalize their capacity to teach into the 'teacher'. So that one is left with a dual absence – there is, through some sort of educational black magic, no one left to do anything with anyone else.

Bourgeois education – and even many who speak of revolution fall into its style – is an elaborately festooned, cheap, circus disappearing act. Or, perhaps better, it is a non-appearance act in which a non-existent magician fails to produce any rabbit out of a hat that is not there either. In terms of an existential algebra, this education is an infinite summation of facts that equals a serial multiplication of negations. The threat posed to authoritarianism by those who revolt against the prevalent forms of sterile academicism in the 'human sciences' resides precisely in an insight into the nothingness that characterizes this aspect of the system, a nothingness that reflects the covert impotence of the whole state structure – a structure which, to extend the metaphor of negation, depends on nothing more than the ultimately counter-productive production of empty stomachs, empty conforming minds, the emptying of guns, the emptying of bomb-compartments over Hanoi and so on. Even to speak of bourgeois power as a paper tiger ascribes too much substance to an impotent nothing. Destruction comes about when we submissively attribute an *unreal* potency to the system. What we have to do then is to discover *our* power that *their* education has made us lose in and between ourselves.

So I would propose books as dialogues in which what goes on in a book becomes a joint creation by all of us.

To refer analogously to the teacher/taught relation I shall quote myself from the transcript of a recent seminar-dialogue I gave in Buenos Aires: 'there is no real need, although there may be a conditioned habit reaction, to maintain the present seating arrangements or our relation to this microphone and so on. The range of transformations of physical and existential space can be seen to be very wide indeed. By existential space I mean a space that cannot be objectively measured and which is defined by the nature of the presence of each person physically here; so that at one time a person may occupy zero existential space by presenting himself as an absence, and at another time he may occupy almost all the "room" by a massive occupation of the interaction that goes on between us. Also some people here may be very familiar with some concepts that come into our discussion, e.g. "double bind", "pseudomutuality", and others less familiar with these concepts although more familiar with other concepts; in such cases someone, by no means necessarily me, who is more familiar with whatever concept could explain it to someone who is less familiar. Of course some of us here have more "experience" of the complexities of what people do to each other, experience that arises not only through years of involvement in the understanding of oneself and others but also – and this may involve much less chronological time – through the rapid development of a sort of epilepsy, which in the original Greek etymological sense meant "seizing upon"; a seizing upon the simple truth of a presented human complexity – a free, spontaneous choice, against all the odds, to know in one gesture of the spirit. To leave this perhaps somewhat esoteric-seeming area there are, I am sure because I am one of them too, many people here who feel that we know nothing and then maybe feel that the knowing that we know nothing may be a necessary no-ing (or negation) of a certain presumption implicit in knowing. We ignorant people and innocent people are the bridge between the people who know (I am, unfortunately, supposed to be one of them too) and the ignorant who exist throughout the world as "the mass of the people". Perhaps finally the masses can exchange some of their nobility, which is really another form of Knowing, for some of the knowledge of the official knowers.

'As I see it we start off by meeting here as some sort of collectivity of people, some of whom know each other or know others who know each other but, essentially, each of us does not know *each* other. At this point, although I am not in accord with him on many other matters, I think that Jean-Paul Sartre's analysis of human meeting and non-meeting (in the *Critique of Dialectical Reason*) usefully simplifies the likely course of events between us. We start off as a serial collectivity, anonymous to each other like people in a bus queue. Then, bit by bit, we sort each other out in terms of fusion or non-fusion into or out of a group. After a certain amount of coming and going we may, hopefully, end up as "*une groupe sermentée*" as Sartre calls it; a group in which we take an oath, which is a concrete metaphor, that commits us to a certain goal-directed activism in the world. This "ending up" is in fact the beginning of an activity that can and will affect many others beyond the initial limited circle. I believe that the main illusion we have to dispel is the illusion of our own impotence. If any one of us talks significantly enough even to one other person, that significance will resonate through the consciousness of dozens, hundreds, thousands of others, by direct contact, and by contact at many removes.

We don't need to present ideas in books, films, television because we have a ready-made medium of communication right here now. *The only true and effective mass-medium is nothing more and certainly nothing less than the mass itself – the mass that we are.* If we do not believe this wholeheartedly enough, that is with a full, encouraging courage, we shall simply submit to our pig masters who lie to us that, at the end of the journey when we have to get out of the cattle-truck at the Destination Camp, we shall be castrated – that is to say become ideally conformist to the system.* Our submission then will mean, as it always has meant, that we walk in orderly file into the gas chambers that we have obediently built for them to asphyxiate their problems in. *Their problems are Us.*' Certainly, to speak of 'them' and 'us' in simple oppositional terms, rather than dialectically – clearly seeing the interdependence and collusions of each with the other – can lead to further violence. But if we fail to see actual, present differences of this sort then the path to revolutionary counter-violence against class and national oppression, ecocide and mind colonization may be impossible to find.

To consent at any moment in any way to the gross or subtle injunctions of the bourgeois system, by specific actions or by the very style of our lives, is to draw the hand of the murderer with its sharp knife across the line of our jugular veins. It's a slow way of dying that can only promise to come too soon.

* By 'the system' I do not refer to an abstraction, The System, but rather to a complex social praxis where people are 'stood together' in such a way that, duly deprived of understanding, they stand being stood together and get others to stand together with them. The epithet 'bourgeois' simply characterizes the authoritarian system in most post-feudal property-owning societies, including some that are supposed to have advanced to socialism.

It would be good now to try to arrive at some consensus on certain questions – questions such as: What is philosophical? What is ideological? and What is the nature of the political? As with most intellectual definitional matters it would be frivolous to spend much time in forming 'water-tight', self-contained definitions at the expense of a proper examination of experience and action themselves; for the latter purpose we need an open-ended, non-obsessional, less cerebrally tight-arsed guide-line to thinking.

Firstly, as I see it, philosophy, as a totalistic attempt to comprehend 'all that is' or the systematic elaboration of principles aimed at such comprehension, is not a possible or desirable enterprise any longer. Any attempt to philosophize in this sense in our age must be stillborn or if it is not it must be therapeutically aborted. On the other hand occidental philosophy has sometimes attempted to encompass, even if often merely to dismiss it, a realm of *experience* called spiritual or mystical (not to be confused with institutionalized religion) that we dare not ignore. The 'spiritual' denotes a central region of experience that at this point in history must no longer be seen as in any way discrepant with the impulse to revolutionary change but rather as an essential experiential component of that will to change. If institutional religion has been 'the opium of the masses', the spiritual is perhaps a drug with quite an opposite effect on action – or, rather than drug, an authentic spirituality is the right sort of experiential food to sustain the right sort of revolutionary action. I believe that this realization has become increasingly clear over the last decade or so. I don't mean marxism plus marijuana or socialist psychedelia, while not decrying this North American tentative, but rather the inspirational acts of the passionate and compassionate revolutionary which cannot be reduced to class conditioning or theoretical political formation.

To proceed, perhaps we shall be able to agree on the meaning of 'the ideological' – I prefer to understand by 'the ideological' 'that which is ideological' rather than Ideology (or for that matter Politics or Philosophy) with capital letters, since we have to avoid dealing with reified abstractions, totally unreal pseudo-entities which are only the symptoms of some sort of non-neurological brain disease which has so long been endemic in academic institutions. 'The ideological', then, as I see it, refers to sets of ideas, sufficiently unified to be practically effective in the world, which are aimed at the transformation of social entities on both the micro-social level (persons, groups of persons) and macro-social level (collectivities, classes, nations) whether for 'better' or 'worse'. Further, that these sets of ideas, which arise from self-directing 'consciousness-praxis' in the world (in the sense in which Sartre sees consciousness and praxis as two sides of the same coin), generate modes of consciousness-praxis that generate further sets of ideas that generate further consciousness-praxis and so on.

The political, as I have said in the introduction, is (or is the study of) the deployment of power in a social entity or between social entities. To deploy power is an activity which involves the disorganization-reorganization of a person, bits of a person or groups or collectivities of people, aimed at some new chosen end. To commence with the micro-political the first area we enter is the *intrapersonal*, our 'insides'. As far as the intrapersonal is concerned we clearly have to include the bodies that we live so that we must see that, for example, the peptic ulcer is a political act too. The myocardial infarct in fact is something that we do to the musculature of our hearts – as if 'our' hearts were properties that we own, properties that we can manipulate like stocks we can exchange on the internal transplantation market. So too are our memories, dreams, phantasy ('unconscious') and fantasies ('conscious'), or whatever we choose to regard as the 'inner life'. I shall return to the notion of 'inner' and 'outer' later in this book when considering the abolition of long-standing notions of 'the Self' and the notion of a responsibility-free 'unconscious'.

Going beyond the individual person the next but interwoven area of the micro-political is the *family-political* area of acts. The bourgeois nuclear family (which in this context I shall henceforth refer to as 'the family') is the principal mediating device that the capitalist ruling class uses to condition the individual, through primary socialization, to fit into some *role complex* that suits the system (the family thus generates a conflict between the active reality of a person and the conditioned passivity of his role complex). This ruling class itself, of course, is most heavily conditioned by the very institution – the family – with which it initiates its destruction of the people it oppresses. Certainly some of one's most centrally important good experiences may occur within the family; I am referring here only to the alienated use of the family in bourgeois society. If we are so conditioned by our family formation it is only too easy to conclude that we are not really responsible for our acts – they all issue ultimately from repressed infantile experience. In capitalist society responsibility is relegated to some increasingly remote authority ending up in a bad, totally alienated madness that is fascism. In present-day versions of fascism the craziness is only slightly less overt than it was in Nazi Germany. The main issue here is the loss of any sense of agency so that no one is experienced as doing anything to anyone except in the most absurdly irrelevant terms. From a totally dehumanized field any sort of inhumanity can arise without question.

If one departs from the pattern of behaviour prescribed for the role complex, certain invalidation operations are performed by the appointed agents of the society, police, militia, educators, psychiatrists, or just ordinary, good, respectable, murderous citizens. This often happens with the active collusion of one's family, particularly in the area of psychiatry where one's nearest and dearest choose to see one as mad and in need of treatment (which = more control) rather than bad – which is the other familiar family path.

LIES.

The next micro-political area is the *face-to-face or confrontation group* that extends beyond the family to include any person or people that one meets and knows, or at least has a chance of meeting or knowing directly. This group of course shows important elements that replicate the family experience of each of its members so that one member may be experienced as infantile or as mothering or fathering in certain previously experienced modes, by another member, etcetera. In the dyadic or polyadic psychoanalytic group this sort of historically mistaken experience is termed transference. The group work in every case must involve, ideally at least, the elimination of illusory family figments so that people face each other as they actually are in the present moment of history-free reality. Personal history is important but important only in so far as its being is being-to-be-transcended now.

OTHERWISE – MORE LIES.

After the micro-political the macro. The transition is important to grasp in experience since the polarization of our lives into micro- or macro-political, each at the expense of the other, is one of the principal divide-and-rule tactics of bourgeois mind-colonization. For instance in a university many students may be very active macro-politically but, like Lenin in relation to Stalin, may ignore what goes on 'under their noses' (I mean Lenin's fatal *personal* non-recognition of Stalin and therefore of Stalin's incipient development of a murderous bureaucracy, although Lenin did belatedly indicate his extreme doubts), while on the other hand some students may develop a highly perceptive awareness of the complexities of their own and other people's behaviour but fail to connect up with a wider-ranging activism. There is no essential antagonistic contradiction between macro- and micro-political activism, between revolutionary socialism and mind-liberation and sexual liberation. On the basis of a recognition, not only of this non-contradictoriness but of interdependence, unity of action is possible.

The phenomenology of the micro-macro transition, the μ-*shift* for short, is next to be examined. The essence of the experience of micro-macro transition is the shift, the μ-shift, from the possibility of working directly on a relationship with another or others in a situation of meeting, to an area of anonymous social organization where some of the people may know some of the others but no one can know all of the others. This latter state of affairs, that emerges from the μ-shift, is a *collectivity*. To put it more precisely one may say that: in the micro-group a person, A, experiences another person, B, who experiences him (A) and A experiences B experiencing him and experiences B's experience of A's experience that B experiences A, and so on. Let arrows represent the direction of experience:

```
A ------▶B

B ------▶A

A ------▶(B ------▶A)

B ------▶[A------▶(B ------▶A)]

C ------▶ A ◀------▶ B ----- ------▶[A------▶(B ------▶A)] etc.
```

In the macro-group collectivity, however, this spiralling internal system is not a structural characteristic of the group and while anyone may experience anyone else this experience remains external unless micro-groups form within the macro-group collectivity and then fully relate to each other. It is important to grasp *in experience* the moment of transition from micro- to macro-grouping and the moment of formation of micro-groups within a macro- context. Otherwise we inevitably flounder in dislocated anonymity and, since we no longer know where we come from, we cannot know where we are; and, because we do not know where we are, we cannot act beyond the limits of an extremely myopic space.

Collectivities may be non-institutional collectivities (which certainly include a number of micro-groups) or institutionalized, for example a trade union, university, political party or church. By institutionalization I mean human grouping in which people are *placed in position* by social processes beyond their individual intentionality; thus one would see bourgeois marriage as an institution in so far as people are conditioned to it by their primary and secondary socialization and submit to legal processes that are alien to their relationship; from the beginning destructive property and money relations are built into the marriage. Sacramental marriage on the other hand is a non-institutional, non-exclusive undertaking to work through all aspects of relationship together, a choice to do this work together that is freely sustained by each of the two or more people involved – it is a movement beyond socialization, a movement out of conditioned being, a movement outside bourgeois law. If we invent an anti-ethic against the bourgeois system we then see sacramental marriage as virtuous whereas legal marriage is highly immoral (our inexperience when some of us fell into it when young only partly excuses us).

There are non-institutional collectivities in which each person chooses to be unified with the others by some more or less specified goal of understanding on the basis of which all can act effectively. Institutionalized collectivities may share this characteristic of an individually chosen common aim but then *sets of rules*, implicit or explicit, determine the position of people within the structure.

In *nation-state politics*, collectivities are organized into a larger entity determined by historical development and geography, in which classes in conflict generate further history. *Geopolitics* is concerned with conflicts between nation-states, international cooperation and also overt and covert imperialism and imperialist war. *Cosmopolitics* is a certain holy madness. It is not *our* madness for we cannot possess it *but it is the madness that we are* unless we fall into the dual trap whereby we elect *either* that we possess it *or* that it possesses us. Cosmopolitics is a numinous politics that exceeds all the categories, and also space and time (as usually understood), that I have used so far.

I realize that I have raised too many questions here, and that we have only a limited time to work our questions out. For instance the bourgeois nuclear family is only one contemporary expression of the family. The original family is the property family long before the bourgeois family – the family in which women become the property of men, children become the property of women and men and all become the property of the slave masters, of feudal barons and clergy and then of the capitalist military-industrial complexes. These last remaining owners of property are themselves owned properties but they don't know who owns them any more than most of the rest of us do. They are the properties of dead leaves of an illusory history book that have lost the beauty of the dead leaves from the tree, they are the properties of abstractions that we have invented as much as them by our complicity with them. The congenitally anomalous child must be saved. The congenitally anomalous abstraction must die because it never lives except through the endless deaths of the people who blindly live by it. There are many strategic bombs that some people will have to place. The one bomb that has never adequately been placed is under the primary mediator of violence that we have to exert our counter-violent might against – the *property-family* and all the false images that would be forms of worship of it.

We have to discover an orang-outang ideal. In its linguistic origins orang-outang means a man from uncultivated parts, archaic regions that antecede in a non-temporal sense our present conditioned states of awareness. This is *nothing like* Rousseau's idea of the noble savage who was supposed to exist externally in the 'past' or 'present' and to which we were hopefully to return.

The orang-outang is a reality hidden within us now. By an act of existential harakiri we have to put our concealed insides out into the world – and stay alive.

In some moments I am tempted to think that life is a boring distraction from death. But dying is *certainly* a boring distraction from life.

So now, with detachment, let us let death die. That is

the most vital political act of all. The political problem is that of achieving a sufficient closeness to our deaths within living experience so that, with our fear well contained, we may lucidly take the simple risks necessary to initiate the complex revolutionary strategies by which we shall free ourselves from the bad habit of consenting to our oppression in class and national terms, and to genocidal ecocide and to the now near final loss of our minds.

2

On Becoming Aware

To eliminate that preposterous, reified, abstract construct 'The Unconscious' – without detracting from its historically limited usefulness – we shall have to deploy simple concepts such as *experience* and *action*. Action here is extended beyond the notion of action in relation to physical presences in the world to include action-on-experience, one's own experience or that of other people.

I have chosen to use the word 'awareness' rather than consciousness in this chapter. Awareness is lexicographically referred to as 'being informed of', or much better, 'a watchful state', while consciousness is defined as awareness but is complicated by the intellectualistic resonances of the Latin derivation *cum + scire* – to know fully. I am 'aware' of the translation difficulties into Latin languages in particular. The Anglo-Saxon origin of awareness is 'gewær' with its relation to the German 'gewahr werden' which is 'becoming true' which is the only true becoming or the only coming into being of truth. 'Consciousness' (English), *conscience* (French), *bewusstsein* (German), *conciencia* or *conocimiento* (Spanish) miss out entirely on the truth level of meaning.* It might then become clear why I have chosen the word awareness, true becoming, as the

* See Walter W. Skeat, *An Etymological Dictionary of the English Language*, The Clarendon Press, Oxford, p. 41.

linguistic expression of pure direction in the sense that I am going to use this term. All talk of 'selves' in relation to 'other selves' is an area for radical demythologization – despite, as I have said, its limited historical utility. For me the notion of awareness-direction will accomplish a requisite demystification. Perhaps a more appropriate word than awareness will occur to you.

Experience comprises primary awareness (A_1) which is relatively pure, neutral, 'in-flow' experience which, in the first instance, is not significantly acted on by secondary awareness. This primary awareness was the original object of phenomenological science. Experience, however, also includes secondary awarenesses (A_2) which are actions upon primary awareness that produce acted-upon or altered primary awarenesses that we may also refer to as A_2 states (so that A_2 refers both to action upon experience A_1 *and* the altered state). A_1 as altered by A_2 refers to what is usually referred to as 'unconscious experience' or 'phantasy'. A_2 is more the normal state of quotidian consciousness although much of A_2 may in fact be suppressed experience – experience suppressed by awareness A_3 (it is important to note that the suppressor act A_3 is merely a convenience of notation – the basic conception is action-on-experience). The notation may run from A_1, A_2, A_3 to infinities of acted-upon experience.

Although I use the term 'repression' in this volume, repression is simply a self-reflexive mode of A_1 acting on itself and has no affinity with the psychoanalytic 'meta-psychological' concept of repression which is an abstraction applied to a supposedly objectifiable psychic apparatus. Suppression is a process in which awareness A_3 acts on A_2 to deflect it into the *mode* of A_1 as altered by A_2 (the altered A_1 then becoming an A_2 awareness). In fact the whole thing devolves onto awareness.

Just because, say, the work done by A_2 on A_1 is 'invisible' it is not abstract or in any sense unreal. It is actual rather in Hegel's sense in which, while reality is what in fact exists, the actual is a reality that has overcome the discrepancy between the possible and the existent. The evidence for the actuality of A_2 work lies both in the *feeling* of work and in the visible consequences in the world, for example the unexpected alteration in the life of another person as a result of certain of one's acts, and in fact any observable issue of reflective behaviour. The reflective action of secondary upon primary awareness may then be actively organized into knowledge (as active awareness not as 'thing') by subsequent reflective acts. Knowledge and, indeed, everything that we have come to regard as our personal mental property is peripheral activity that points towards and specifies the nothing of the zero-self.

When we speak of A_2 we refer to an identity of experience and action, the altering awareness A_2 is both experience-action and its results and the awareness of its results – although it may be merely convenient to refer to the latter as A_3 (and thereby extend the notion of A_2) and to the further act of experiencing the action on experience of actions as A_4 and so on. At this particular point in the elaboration of the argument I would admit an indebtedness, with some important modifications, to Sartre's unified concept of consciousness-praxis that he expounds throughout the *Critique of Dialectical Reason*.

The key idea underlying this argument is the very simple one that is at the heart of Husserl's original phenomenological science, that there is no consciousness that is not a consciousness-of something, that there is an organic link between consciousness and its object. Otherwise we would be left with a 'property' state of affairs in which we 'had' a consciousness which 'had' its object. A great deal of metaphysical speculation has been based on this property-orientated view of mind and therefore has been vitiated by this non-consciousness of its own history. To take a simple example, a man has passive sexual feelings towards another man (intentional object inseparable from the sexual feeling). This is awareness A_1 which is acted upon by the culturally conditioned awareness A_2 to produce the altered experience whereby the first man feels that the second man wants to fuck him up. The condition A_1 may be 'historically' linked with previous awarenesses both A_1 and A_2 in relation to the first man's father in which the latter featured both as a 'negative' person and as the object of passive homosexual wishes (A_1 altered by A_2). Further reflective awareness may decondition the cultural distortion of experience to allow a liberating recognition of the primary feeling, so that one is free to act or not to act from that feeling according to the totality of one's primary desires and one's possibilities.

To elaborate a non-property-orientated view of how 'minds' relate to 'their objects' the idea I would propose is that of *direction*. Unfortunately, we probably cannot yet, unlike certain tribes, dispose of all talk of 'minds', 'ideas in (occupying or occupied) minds', 'the self', 'inner' and 'outer' and so on. We can, however, lay the foundations of a mode of experiencing that would dispose of these obfuscating constructs. Direction is from the Latin *directus*,* straight, the passive past participle of *dirigere*, to straighten, from the Latin *di* (for *dis*), apart, and *regere*, to rule, control. I would like to develop a connotation of discipline as a primary, definitive character of direction, rather than control in the compulsive, everyday

* For example, Skeat, *An Etymological Dictionary of the English Language.*

sense. Direction eludes the aprioristic Kantian forms of thought, space and time, as well as his categories. Direction does *not* imply the relation of two points in time or any relation of time to the relation of those points. It is only the mind that Kant was analysing that would suppose such relations. For a notation for direction we may use lines with arrowheads but this is only a makeshift concession to the Kantian or neo-Kantian minds that we have been taught we 'possess'.

In some of the psychoanalytic literature we find a further confusion that needs clarification, which means elimination, and that is talk of a 'conscious self' and 'unconscious self', so that we have to examine notions of self. Self is often conveniently defined as 'one's own person' whereas 'person' illuminatingly refers to 'character, individual, body' with a secondary Latin reference to 'a mask' (of?). The Middle English usage of self emphasized constancy, 'same or very'. Here the notion of constancy subserved the property ideal in a feudal time expressed as the *owning* of one's own self. The basic issue is the inextricable linking of *substantialistic concepts of self* and *property*.

In one and the same philosophical act we have to rid ourselves of the idea of self and of simplistic notions of space and time, without falling into idealism as A. N. Whitehead did when he attacked the idea of simple location, and also avoiding the neo-neo-platonic idealism of his attacks on the 'fallacy of misplaced concreteness'. To do this, one of the weapons we shall use, consequent upon the primary notion of direction, is that of *spaces* that do not exist 'in' space but which are defined as non-spatial *places* by directions. Directions are not 'of' anything nor made of anything, they are rather specific nothings that are the meaning of the being that they fracture.

So the notion of specificity is part of the notion of direction. Despite appearances no two directions of awarenesses are the same. The facts of mind and body are simply different sorts of spaces (specific nothings) defined as places by directions (other specific nothings). I admit to having used ideas of history in this book but such time-notions again are simply different sorts of spaces defined as places by directions.

Experiences with Lysergic Acid Diethylamide helped me beyond measure to realize these non-spatial and non-temporal spaces that can never be in physical space since they issue from nothingness of directions. One may learn with LSD (which is only one amongst many other 'breakthrough' experiences) the possibility of entering spaces that are outside our culturally 'emplaced' biological life-histories. Places before our births and beyond our deaths. We may learn, using the time-language that our Kantian minds have been falsely taught to use, how to enter into post-death and pre-birth spaces during our chronological life span and we may know 'during our lives' what, for example, these after-death and pre-birth spaces are like – hence the inestimable value of LSD or LSD-equivalent experiences for people confronted with the imminent possibility of biological death, and hence its importance both for the revolutionary – who faces torture and death – and the person dying of an incurable disease. Hence also its supreme importance for those who wish to enter and know the spaces that are called 'mad'. The organicity of the relation of madness to post-death and pre-birth experience is illuminated by LSD and related substances which are not on any account to be regarded as 'drugs', but rather as spiritual food.* I shall

* One might reflect on the idea that most occidental philosophy (after the gnostics and pre-socratics and excepting thinkers like

illustrate this later but first I would like to make more graphically clear the relation of A_1 to A_2 and the definition of places by directions.

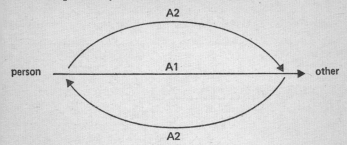

Firstly let us use constructs that have to be eliminated, I mean those of 'the person' (who masks nothing) and 'the other' (who similarly is a non-existent mask of nothing). Let us use these ideas in parentheses.

The 'person' experiences the 'other' but simultaneously acts on the primary awareness ('unconscious' in general) which is returned as a secondary awareness ('consciousness' in general). Also each experience the person has is bidirectional – it acts on the person who is experiencing-acting. The space that awareness directions create that we refer to as 'The Self' (or the mind or the

---

Eckhart, Pascal, Nietzsche, Heidegger) is the result of a culturally conditioned constriction of the visual field of the metaphysical eye with biochemical correlates that suggest a literal, culturally intelligible poisoning of our bodies. Much systematic philosophy might then be seen as a dis-ease of our bodies more than a disease of language. A transformation of the way in which we have come to live our 'normal' bodies, 'mediating' normal experience to our normal minds, may be more relevant than a therapy of language. *Systems* of philosophy, as distinct from philosophizing acts, may be seen as different syndromes due to poisons we have taken into ourselves – poisons that range from plastic food to the grotesqueries of social modes of relationship and the fetishized commodity and the trivial spectacle.

27

body) is a nothing that we may indicate, though of course not depict, diagrammatically.

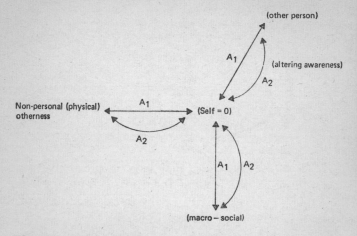

Diagram of the Zero Self

It is important to note in the diagram that the altering (the arrowheads indicate alteration even if the alteration is the negative work of keeping it the same) designated by the A_2 line alters the alterer much as awareness A_1 alters the alterer. One might say, then, that there is no self but only directional self-alteration.

It may be argued that in using historical concepts like 'the result of' our philosophically indoctrinated minds accept limitation by language and one cannot always use inverted commas. Ideas of development, process, dialectical change are not time dependent. *Truly time Is.* The generation of history is the direction or redirection of directions, the 'simultaneous' awarenesses A_1 and A_2 are the moment of alteration that is history. So, too, thesis-antithesis-synthesis is the historical moment which has no relation to the moments of history measured in clock-time. The action of *putting the past behind as past and putting the future ahead as future is a present act*. If one's awareness expands as in mystical experience or with LSD-like substances, this all becomes clear and obvious and philosophically indoctrinated space-time concepts disappear in the moment of realization of their essential illusoriness. This is indeed the supreme, liberating cathartic experience.

What I am saying does not depend on the presence on the scene of aware human subjects. Pre-human history is a directed structuring *of the present*. This is merely *how* prehistory happens and does not make it any the less 'real' for all that.

The only valid death wish now is death to substantialistic illusions of a self located in measurable space and time. The specific zero self is one with all.

3

The Acid Test

In this chapter I am writing not only, as might be supposed from the title, about certain anti-drugs such as LSD, mescaline, psilocybin, 581* and so on, but about critical ecstatic experiences in general; experiences that test out the value for living of all the previous conditioned experiences we have accumulated. This testing becomes critical when we begin to ask whether it is in fact worth going on living at all with that opaque mass of conditioning through which no light may ever show.

By ek-stasis I mean standing outside 'one's' 'self' through a prior *anoia* or cancelling out of 'our' conditioned 'minds'. There is of course an ecstasy of religious and aesthetic experience that is arrived at, to put it nonreductively in terms of its physiological correlates, by an experientially triggered internal chemical change rather than by ingesting chemicals. There are in fact many paths to ecstasy and these paths are by no means mutually exclusive. The tradition is very ancient, going back to Neolithic shamanism as well as the shamanism that more recently existed in Tibet and became involved with the

* 581 is a substance originally used in anaesthesia but recently employed in Buenos Aires to produce a pure, relatively content-free 'regression' (unlike LSD) lasting some 5–8 hours. My experiences with these substances during 1972 were wholly positive in terms of a most radical destructuring-restructuring of awareness.

meditation on Mahayana Buddhism to China and Japan, as well as the shamanism probably still extant in Mongolia and Eastern Siberia, the Andes and so on. Also to the certainly still extant, verbally uncommunicable rituals of the esoteric 'left-handed' *tantra*. Further, the paths to ecstasy in this sense go back (or forward?) to other animals; for instance the satori of the large primates nearest to man and the way that gorillas in conflict simply 'stare each other out' rather than fight. Lest any one feel disposed to take what I say sarcastically or with a light, unenlightened heart, let me say now without irony that there is a serious mathematics behind all that I say. This is a mathematics of non-metric topology, of pure direction: direction in which the only residual parameter is that of continuity-discontinuity-continuity. It is a mathematics of self-directing generalization which needs treatment in another volume. To illustrate some of the points I wish to make I shall report an experience related to me by a very close friend.

'One day when I was working, a young woman, who seemed to know me although I did not know her, came to the front door. Without words we embraced and seemed to know that now was "the moment". She produced 300 micrograms of LSD for each of us and silently and sacramentally we took it. We took off our clothes and lay on the bed. We then got into a "left-handed" tantric sexual *yoga* in which the female and male body elements became One. This was in the first three quarters of an hour although clock-time only assumed significance in retrospect. "I" experienced an orgasm that spiralled off through infinities of time and had no end – like all the rest of the experience it remains with me now as a permanent alteration. Then I experienced from some remote point in physical space (that was really a place in the directional sense I have tried to explain in the previous chapter) an immense cosmic cataclysm in which whole galaxies turned brown and black and were torn asunder by blinding white forces of light. After aeons of time spent in this state I started falling into a deep pit, at the distant bottom of which was a brown disc through which I would fall if I did not stop myself. This indicates the discipline that is possible with acid – the discipline by which one can limit the experience of terror, in fact the most central fact about acid is the acquisition of a power that can *de-terrorize* death, madness and any experience of ultimate disaster. So that these experiences, rather than being suppressed, can become part of a fullness of being. I decided that unlike in certain dreams, in which one wakes up before reaching the bottom of the hole, or in which one grabs hold of some secure enough promontory at the side of the pit, I would carry on falling to the limit. I fell through the brown disc *into nothing*. I was in a state in which there was no "I" to experience the nothing – just pure nothing, nowhere and beyond any sense of time. I don't know if I was biologically dead on the "outside" in this time. It was death as a space beyond where we are now – but which we can experience something of *now*. After the nothing I became a crouched ape-like stone effigy which gradually moved into life as the "space-time me". I then experienced a rush of "paranoid" fantasies in which I felt that the police had entered the room and that I was about to be "busted" on every conceivable, fantastic, or not so fantastic, charge – anarchistic politics, every sort of sexual deviation, every sort of drug offence. I was completely alone in this as my partner had, non-literally, disappeared, but I knew enough from previous acid voyages to "go along with" this experience and not to turn it off because of fear.

'At this point I had to decide to turn off the acid experience for a while because, together with other members of the commune I was living in, I had a premonition that something terrible was happening to one of our comrades who lived down the road. We all rushed out to see him and found that he had taken a large dose of weed-killer. He had to be rushed to hospital and was then pronounced to be in a non-critical state. I then resumed my voyage and, after about five hours, I experienced a beatific vision of an old man with a long beard sitting on a hill with a little boy, suffused with a blue light surrounded by a golden aureola. The boy was holding out his hand to receive manna from heaven, and I then knew that in whatever state, "dead" or "alive", and in difficulties, the gift of that vision would always come to me. I retain that beatific vision with undiminished force.'*

I want to emphasize that LSD is no easy short-cut to mystical experience or, for that matter, to the work that is done in psychoanalysis (when it achieves, as it rarely does, the quality of non-alienated therapeutic exchange) – work that happens largely in spite of the formal context of psychoanalysis. The LSD experience is light-years away from the psychoanalytic. It is very hard spiritual work to acquire the discipline of the experience before new places outside space and time can be navigated. It may therefore be appropriate at this point to define the conditions of a good voyage.

1. The voyage should be undergone in a place one is familiar with and comfortable in. Needless to say, this is extremely difficult in a clinic or any sort of medical setting.

* This beatific vision was a 'protector' place that will always counteract the evil-self places that I shall describe later.

2. The time in one's life to embark on such a voyage needs much experience to judge. Suffice it to say that LSD is not a substance to be taken at difficult times to resolve crises. One should be ready for a major change in life but have an almost routine, automatic system of activity aimed at survival in the world 'ticking over' but with a clear three days for the trip and its immediate after-work – no immediately pressing practical decisions or problems or other exacting or alienating commitment, for example.

3. The trip should be taken with someone experienced in the use of acid, who is able to participate fully in the experience with one (though someone else in the house may not be on acid but can keep at bay interference such as the telephone or door-bell – at least during the eight main hours of the trip). The other person on acid, the 'trip guide', should be cool enough not to try prematurely to bring one down from a so-called 'bad trip' by chlorpromazine (largactil, thorazine), etc. – because no trips are 'bad' unless they are aborted by bad interference. The sinister and horrifying experiences become containable, given the right context, and can be integrated with the 'good' experiences.

I am aware that in saying much of what I am saying I am making proposals that are at present beyond the law in many countries. Those countries will need a bit of political up-dating. In particular I refer to the trip guide as a person experienced in the use of acid (and in their own madness). I do not refer to a professional (e.g. medical) person for the simple reason that 'the profession of being a person' is an impossible career in principle. In England, however, LSD can only be administered legally by medical practitioners.

In the USA there is a Federal Food and Drug Administration. On the principle of forming anti-governments I would suggest the formation of a Federal, and later International, Spiritual, Food and Drug Authority; that would cut through many repressive barriers. LSD and LSD-like substances and cannabis may be more appropriately regarded as food but, as with other foods, a certain dietary discretion is necessary, and in the present state of our civilization we may need expert guidance regarding what foods we ingest and when, since we have long forgotten what is 'good' for us. Foods, however, are essentially life-enhancing, whereas drugs include substances that destroy our bodies and constrict our experience – heroin, alcohol, barbiturates and amphetamines and the massive, indiscriminate use of other poisons in psychiatric 'treatment'. Probably both in third- and first-world countries cannabis should remain illegal. The pay-off of this is that more revolutionary potential is mobilized and more and more people acquire the requisite 'paranoia' (i.e. alertness) about police intervention, and this alertness is useful for other activities. Also, as Frantz Fanon wrote, cannabis can delay revolutionary action. LSD, taken by certain people at the right time and in the right context, can more deeply mobilize revolutionary potential – especially in terms of the acquaintanceship with post-death spaces that can prepare one for the risks that an activist must eventually run. Ultimately, as we revolutionize our 'psycho-chemistry' and our lives, substances like LSD will become superfluous. For the time being, in pre-revolutionary society, the careful use of such substances by certain persons under strictly observed conditions may facilitate personal revolution, which can be integrated into the wider context of liberation of the society.

4. The LSD should be chemically pure, obviously not completely phoney, or adulterated with 'speed' (amphetamines) as is so often the case. The optimum dosage for most people is between 100 and 300 micrograms. Massive dosage beyond 300 micrograms is pointless as one simply achieves a negative perceptual shattering. Unlike Timothy Leary and his associates, for whose work I have much respect, I believe that if one is going to do anything with acid it can be done with 100 micrograms or even less – depending on the state one's life is in.

5. The place for the experience should be completely warm so that one and one's partner can get rid of clothing in order to experience one's body more fully. Sexuality may or may not be indicated according to the wishes and the life-timing of the experience for each person involved. An obvious contradiction here is that medical doctors, who are the only legal source of LSD (in England in 1974), are limited by their professional rules from full participation in the experience.

6. Although I have referred to the danger of a panic-stricken partner bringing one down by the anxious use of phenothiazines, after five–eight hours of a trip, it may be in order to quell the occasional post-voyage muscular fibrillation and agitation (which may occur mildly even when the context has been good) by taking a (literal) drug. For this purpose medical prescription is necessary; barbiturates are not advisable, as these produce a bad 'down' apart from being addictive. It is ironic that alcohol and nicotine are freely available and barbiturates and amphetamine are freely available on prescription, while all are addictive drugs – like heroin or methadone (a 'treatment' for heroin addiction). Cannabis and LSD are physically non-addictive yet against the law in most

countries. The myths of LSD causing brain damage, chromosomal damage or foetal abnormalities if taken during pregnancy have been effectively dismissed,* though I have mentioned my beliefs about the negative perceptual shattering of high dosage and, as regards pregnancy, I believe that that experience should be sufficiently replete with ecstasy for LSD to be contra-indicated.

7. One must be aware of the limitations of 'pre-programming', e.g. my experience of a series of suburban housewives in a psychiatric context to whom a psychiatrist gave LSD lead me to believe that the culturally conditioned experience of being a suburban housewife could simply be intensified by a 'non-trip'. It is certainly possible for the experience to be turned off entirely and from the beginning. Normal control of one's experience may be fully retained unless avoidable negative factors in the human situation lead one to panic. It is desirable, however, that control should be relinquished and replaced by a very clear *discipline* by which one allows in as much fearful experience as one can deal with at one time.

8. I would emphasize one real danger of the Acid Voyage and that is the *mobilization of destructive selves*, usually described as 'auto'-destruction. These essentially mythic selves are *in* us but not of us. I use the false language of internalization and externalization, but this is significantly better than psychoanalytic talk of 'mechanisms' of introjection and projection – significantly better since it refers to experience-acts rather than to quasi-objective mechan-

* See J. C. Lilly, *The Center of the Cyclone*, Julian Press, New York, 1972, p. 81 ff. And papers of the Spring Grove State Hospital LSD research group by Drs Walter Pahnke, Stanislaf Grof, Charles Savage and Albert Kurlard from the Maryland Psychiatric Research Center, Catonsville Md.

isms. The destructive selves or evil places may take over and after the trip may seriously damage one – the mythic entities lead to non-mythic effects in the world. In the trip one begins to recognize good and evil protectors that one can increasingly rely on or not rely on. The destructive selves are essentially alien internalizations of bad aspects of one's parents and others or of evil cosmic forces. This is where we begin to speak of *cosmopolitics* as distinct from family politics or nation-state politics. The self-destruction may be acted out literally or metaphorically. One may 'accidentally' burn one's self to death or do so metaphorically. The only answer to the problem of destructive selves is a good enough acquaintance with good enough protector selves. There is no guarantee in the voyage about this. For example the mythic self* of 'the alcoholic' that makes the alcoholic drink – a self that may be entirely non-syntonic with the rest of the person – may be revealed in a more naked form with LSD and may assume a different character. This is where psychoanalysis, or rather therapy, in the good sense I attempt to clarify in this book, and adequate preparation and care after the voyage – *the total context* – come in. The dangers are avoidable.

Finally, I feel that at this time ultimate mergence with the Clear Light of the Void is an historical impossibility and would in fact be a betrayal of the revolutionary imperative. We have therefore to make a lucid internal promise before the voyage to return to the world transformed so that we can help transform the world.

* This mythic 'self' is expressed by the second line of the Japanese saying:

> A man takes a drink
> The drink takes a drink
> The drink takes the man.

4

An Orgasm Manifesto

Why orgasm, which seems to be an individual duo act, should be regarded as political is an easily answerable question if one accepts my previous definition of 'the political'. Every 'significant experience' is orgasmic in minuscule or majuscule. By 'significant experience' I mean experience that alters a person's life or alters the history of the world, or anywhere between – and altering involves the deployment of power. It is experience that involves the critical emptying of one's mind – the bold negation of consciousness – death in life, and then the restructuring of a renewed awareness. This is accomplished by any effective art form and is certainly at the heart of revolutionary activism – it is only by negating all previous security devices in one's life that one may perform a revolutionary task. The no-mind centre of orgasm is a training in death experience for the revolutionary, as well as being the centre of a transforming joy.

Another reason why orgasm is politically important is that it represents, in a pre-revolutionary context, a breakdown of repressive barriers – barriers that can destroy a revolution based by its theoreticians on a simplistic economism, on a change in the ownership in the means of production and relations of production, from which, it is hoped, all else will automatically ensue. Removal of superficial repressive barriers by the liberalization of sexual mores may make for an easy-going promiscuity that masks a far deeper repression – *the repression of orgasmic ecstasy* which differentiates making love from fucking, in which each is reduced to a sexual object by the other. The message must be bread *and* orgasm – otherwise one can live but live for nothing, one can create a revolution that finally is not worth having. The leitmotiv is orgasm as much as possible by any means possible within the context of non-possessive love. This by no means implies a disregard of individual persons with whom one may wish for a unitary orgasmic couple. A multiplication of the possibilities of love does not imply anonymizing 'promiscuity'. It is hackneyed to say that a joy that surpasses delight and a glory that surpasses laudation are at the centre of revolution. By joy I mean a new awareness that palpates the heart of orgasm in that centre. The revolutionary act embodies itself to produce a no-mind state. *That* is orgasm too. The operation of minds comes before and after the ecstatic moment.

Orgasm has become the most mystified state of feeling. No one can be quite sure if they 'have' it or not. Is it just ejaculation or is it orgasm? Is it just involuntary pelvic contractions or is one 'having' orgasm?

The first step towards demystification is ridding 'oneself' of *property attitudes*; this is by no means simple and has to be lived out fully in one's everyday life. For some middle-class people for instance it may mean reducing one's needs, say, to a double mattress on the floor, the means of making coffee and the simplest food, as well as a change from parasitic occupation to productive work.* No luxu-

* It is necessary at this point to judge whether one is in a parasitic occupation or doing productive work: if one concludes the

ries. The life of a voluntary cell. The second step is to look the other in the face and dare to be looked at. One can always diagnose the non-orgasmic personality by minute ocular deflections and by sentences spoken to one that fail to connect because they are never properly ended. When one looks the other in the eye there is a further possible mystification because one can look the other in the eye without seeing the other. A further step, that may or may not be necessary in practice, is to be able to masturbate the other or oneself or help the other to masturbate herself or himself or oneself with full visual contact – both eye-to-eye contact and eye-to-genital contact.*

Orgasm is a time-less moment in which an excess of vitality (body) generates death (no-mind as opposed to the sense of mind as a 'head' hegemony that subjugates and would annihilate lower body centres) on the way to renewed life. The female way of getting pleasure, moving in a certain manner, voluntarily at first then involuntarily, corresponds to the muscular dance of male ejaculation. Orgasm, however, involves not only this but also infinitely more. In orgasm there is a moment in which pleasure vanishes along with any sense of boundaried self – there 'is' nothing. This is the essential relation between death and orgasm and other ecstatic states at their central moment. The prerequisite of orgasm is a love relationship (whether the relationship be for fifty years or five hours) in which we can trust the other enough to give up one's self image† and the image of one's

_____

latter it might be worthwhile to have second thoughts about what the product really is.

   * Of course blind people can have orgasm too: who said we have only two eyes? Looking, in the sense intended here, is not reducible to the contents of visual fields.

   † Please note that in using linguistic notions like 'one's self

body, in particular one's face, to the other. This is why it is so essential to orgasm to look the other in the eye – to see and to be seen by the other. Given such trust one can give up one's body and self images to the other while simultaneously being reassured of recovering these aspects of one's self. On the basis of trust the major fear that orgasm may lead to the loss of self in a wild and final madness can be overcome. Trust guarantees 'the return'.

We can now try to answer some frequent questions: Can only one person of a couple making love have orgasm? Yes, as long as the self can be given up totally to the other on a particular occasion, which may be reversed on another occasion: this is why many sexual difficulties can be resolved if, as I have indicated, one can as an 'introduction' masturbate or be masturbated while being watched by the other. This is quite often a necessary therapeutic move, although far more important is simply to increase the intensity of eye-to-eye exchange. Can one achieve orgasm by masturbation? Yes, but rarely, if one can conjure up the sense of another who watches one intently enough with some strong remembered feeling of trust; for the most part masturbation produces only the pleasurable body component of orgasm without the experience. Can one have orgasm with only one particular other person whom one loves? No, orgasm in the full sense should be possible with more than the particular other. While orgasm is essential to love it is not coincident with love for only one central other. In fact orgasm with the person one is most centrally working on a relationship with may have to be preceded by orgasm with others in the course of that central relationship.

image' I am not introducing a property notion: there can be 'experience of self image as possessed', but there can be no 'one's self' that 'one' possesses (see Chapter 2).

Each of Wilhelm Reich's criteria for orgasm can now be seen to be false (despite my profound respect for Reich's work in general): (1) that orgasm has to be, it is implied, heterosexual (I deal with this in the next few pages); (2) that there must be no irrelevant fantasies (these in fact may be *necessary* and experientially enriching, and one should be able to speak of them to one's partner or partners without deceit); (3) that orgasm must be of 'appropriate duration' (in experiential fact orgasm can take either a second or aeons of time); (4) that, above all, orgasm must result in a complete release of 'damned-up libido' (this absurd and irrelevant reduction of experience to metric, 'economic' terms is a false mode of pseudo-explanation that does violence to the purely qualitative nature of the experience).

Moreover, release of the 'orgasm reflex' by working on taut muscular structures in the consulting room in a unidirectional doctor-patient context disastrously dissociates orgasm from love. Certainly the genital mechanisms of orgasm may be brought into play but there is no relinquishing of one's self and body image to the regard of a trusted other which is at the heart of love. It is simply a cheap (and costly) substitution of orgasm-mechanism, mere fucking for orgasm-experience as revolving around, revolutionizing and being revolutionized by love.

The question of feigning orgasm is not simply a masochistic device on the woman's part to deceive and gratify the man by reassuring him of his virility, but the man feigns that *he* has had orgasm because she 'has', although she has had 'it' no more than he has. It becomes more complex when she has to pretend that she has not noticed that he has not noticed her pretence to him. Through this complex mystification her pretence to him can be translated in her inner language into 'now I've really had an orgasm!' whereas the man at his end of the transaction reads the message as 'I've given her an orgasm – great!' And in this market for counterfeit notes he may conclude that he has had an orgasm too – even a 'simultaneous orgasm'. The pay-off in the area of orgasm is awe-inspiring. It is as if whole lives depend for their existence on a quotidian (or once a week or fortnight) treachery. There are needless to say many large families in which the parents have never experienced orgasm, since there is no necessary relation between procreation and sexual experience.

At this point let me repeat that orgasm is a matter of the right involuntary pelvic muscular contractions and, at the apex, a state of no-mind – very much like in an epileptic fit though of course not with the same sequence of events. Bearing this in mind, we are led to note that *in fact male orgasm is even less frequent than female orgasm – which is rare enough anyhow* (in the first-world bourgeoisie and in the bourgeoisified elements of first-world working class and the third world).* This must have some relation to the fact that men make slower changes in therapy than women, in general, because therapy should involve orgasmic moments; the exception being men already well in touch with their female aspect and overtly homosexual men once they realize that the therapist is not trying to 'convert' them sexually – or in the fact that the therapist is able to see homosexuality not as a disease but rather the lack of adequate homosexual experience as the disease. This goes along with the view of therapy as being a Big Fuck (*mutual* penetration of the being of each other by the being of the other) rather than the usual sort of fuck-up.

* Mere pleasurable ejaculation is not orgasm. Reich was correct in differentiating erectile and ejaculatory potency from orgastic potency. Instant erections, frequently revived, only too often mask total impotence as far as orgasm is concerned.

One of the most bitter paradoxes one may have to face is that often one does not experience orgasm with the individual one loves most but only with relatively un-involved persons. This is no argument for 'promiscuity' but rather means the right sort of work in therapy (I do not refer to formal, clinical therapy with an 'official' therapist, but to a healing relationship, aimed at a rigorous demystification of all elements of personal reality – this therapy is always mutual though one person for a certain time may need it more than the other). The therapist and 'therapeutized' achieve orgasmic moments of insight – though this may sometimes, at the right time, involve jealousy-free physical relations too. All I can do is to reassure you from my own experience that such jealousy-free moments are possible. It's a matter of trust in the therapist (who in turn trusts the other) and knowing through a sufficiency of trust that it's 'all for the best'.

All previous psychoanalytic theories about the vaginal orgasm as representing sexual 'maturity' in women are, as is well known, overthrown.* The clitoris reigns supreme. But there is more to it than that. The principal erotic zone in women involves also the labia minora and much more tissue around the clitoris that indirectly stimu-lates the clitoris when friction is applied. Compared to the penis and under-surface of the glans of the penis this means that *women have much bigger 'penises' than men*. The 'castration complex' has truly been put in reverse. Nor is it only a question of erotogenic 'size'. A woman may have up to five orgasms in the course of one penile pene-tration, i.e. until the male ejaculates, but may have up to

* For an excellent treatment of female sexuality that develops into regions of biology and greatly extends the work of Masters and Johnson, see Mary Jane Sherfey, *The Nature and Evolution of Female Sexuality*, Random House, New York, 1972.

fifty orgasms in an hour. This would *seem* to mean that, in one sense, for the fullest gratification, a woman needs many men or a great deal of masturbation. Men need to learn how much pleasure they might obtain by masturbating a woman before and after the primary act of making love. It is possible that men through varying contact with the woman's body after ejaculation may greatly increase their capacity to regain penile erection – the myth of inevitable detumescence is based on the cultural notion that men must come back from 'work' (the job) to 'come' very much. I hope, however, that no one believes that I am prescribing fifty orgasms an hour as a necessity for anyone.

How different this is from psychoanalytic statements by *women* such as Helene Deutsch who gave her opinion that the most 'feminine' type of orgasm is one with no orgastic component at all, but one having a passive-receptive, sucking-in action, ending in a mild, slow relaxation which brings 'complete gratification'.

On the question of homosexual orgasm one can only say that this is clearly possible in terms of the relinquishing of one's body image to a trusted other. Moreover, in the male case (in the female case orgasm through mutual clitoral stimulation is obvious), the prostatic area is a principal erotogenic zone and is the one way that male erotogenesis in the genital area can significantly extend beyond the penile limits. It seems significant to me incidentally, in relation to this, that men so often shut off their anuses to female digital penetration. In talking to very many heterosexual, bisexual (which merely means that the person experiences sexuality with people of both sexes), and homosexual men, a certain consensus seems to emerge: prostatic stimulation whether by the fingers of a woman or by the fingers or penis/penises of another man/

men extends male zonal erotogenesis producing a prolongation of penile erection, and intensification of the neuro-muscular mechanism of orgasm and increased frequency of the operation of the mechanism. Also anal exploration whether alone or with others is an essential part of total body exploration. For men, and I am concentrating on the male position here since men on the whole seem more in need of enlightenment about orgasmic sexuality than women, anal stimulation is one part of one path leading to full orgasmic experience; it is, however, only one path and like all the paths to the neuro-muscular mechanism of orgasm it is by no means essential for total orgasmic experience in love that transcends the basic physiology. For men, other paths to orgasm may involve for instance a variety of extra-genital contacts with a woman – penile contact via her mouth, anus, inter-mammary and axillary contact, contact with her lower abdomen and so on. The man internalizes these areas of the woman's body so that they become additional erotogenic zones *inside himself*. Such reinforcement of the man does not imply appropriation from the woman. It is not a zero sum situation.

In the course of the movement into orgasm extra-genital forms of sexual relating liberate the bodies of both for the full experience of penile-vaginal contact in the heterosexual case. For both women and men the experience of the progressively less inhibited, growing excitement of the other becomes an essential part of the voyage into orgasm. The intermingling of skin and oral secretions (also urinary and anal excretions and menstruation), the smearing and tactile feeling of genital secretions on the lower abdomen, face, lips and other parts of the body, the smell and taste of these secretions, are all ports of call on the voyage. Yet many liberated men cannot look, much less lovingly look, the vagina of the woman 'in the eye', much less locate and stimulate her clitoris and periclitoral tissue in a mutually satisfying way, or simply ask her how she likes to be touched; nor can the woman sort her way through her taboos to do similar things with him. Non-vaginal-penile sexuality is usually put down as 'vicarious' – it certainly can be a matter of being 'instead of' but far more importantly it is a necessary journey that leads into full genital orgasm unless there is a failure of nerve on the part of one or both. This failure of nerve leads to grotesqueries such as the woman shaving hair off her legs and armpits and being ashamed of the man playing with and smelling her menstrual secretions, and the use of deodorants by either, or some men's routine of washing their penis after making love, or the woman not knowing what to do with semen in her mouth.

Next there is the illusory idea of certain forms of sexuality being *passive*, such as being 'sucked off' by the mouth of the other or either's anal penetration by the other. This 'passivity', 'passive' heterosexual or homosexual experience with the other, is a sheer myth based on the illusion that women are passive or minimally mobile in penile-vaginal intercourse – disastrously often reinforced in fact by the body, especially hands, arms and weight in front-to-front love-making with the man on top holding the woman in a fixed position to fearfully avoid the beautiful, frenetic, uncontrolled movements of her body in full, free sexuality. This loss of control through free movement of wild intensity is seen as a dangerous madness and a complete loss of self which may be unrecoverable and accounts for the usual confinement of sexuality to within the pre-orgasmic limits. But of course only too often the woman who experiences this loss of control apologizes, saying she 'feels so ashamed', like the man who tries to inhibit the natural sounds of love-making. Also the illusion, religiously indoctrinated, that sex must be a rare, non-excessive penile-vaginal activity aimed at procreation, with a bit of pleasure but never joy, eludes a real happening: the stirring of the anaesthetic neck of the woman's womb (and upper two thirds of the vagina) by the end of the man's penis stimulates all the surrounding pelvic tissues and resonates through to the fully sensory-supplied parts of the lower abdomen, with accompanying mutual fantasies of her impregnation. This of course in itself does not activate the neuro-muscular centre of orgasm but is a necessary extended component of the experience if it is to become total.

The simplistic view that the man is there to penetrate the woman is a culturally conditioned belief that is readily contradicted by experience. Tantric *yoga* is centred on *mutual* penetration, and in true orgasm the penetrator/penetrated opposition is overcome at the climactic moment. Today we recognize the woman's clitoris and periclitoral zone as penetrating, also, secondly, the woman's whole body may become experienced as a penis – this is the true sense of the 'phallic woman' (*not* a woman's body with an illusory penis stuck on). Thirdly, the feeling quality of the woman's body, which is more extensive and sensitive than the man's restricted work-time-controlled mind and body, may be more emotionally penetrating than the man's. Instead of '*vive la différence*' the slogan today is becoming more like '*la différence au potin!*' I think, however, that the relation between these positions is dialectical rather than an opposition.

Orgasm as the fulfilment of love is a form of work that takes most of us a long time to carry through to indefinitely surpassable limits – limits that perpetually exceed prior limits. But it is work that is endlessly delightful and need never be arduous. We have to become *conquistadores* in new territories without ever wreaking violence against that which was there before – all previous experiences with the same person or other people.

The first notes of the overture to subsequent orgasm are struck when one is very small. The mother who masturbates her infant son 'to stop him crying' is in fact also *creating* a shared pleasure. The little girl of five years who can experience the full nerve-muscle component of orgasm (as has been clearly demonstrated neuro-physiologically) must not, for the sake of a germinal love, be denied such an experience. 'Ageism', legally enshrined moralistic prohibitions against sexuality according to age, must be demythologized as urgently as 'sexism'. Initiation of young children into orgasmic experiences, in spontaneous body-exploration and play within their peer-group, will become, I believe, part of a full education towards the end of this century. This is quite opposite to the prevalent 'theft of childhood' – girls of ten training for their use as family commodities, using make-up and so on – and goes along with the possibility of extending the quality of childhood experience into all later stages of life. Revolutionary education destroys game-playing with the weapon of play. So, too, women's liberation and gay liberation have become movements stirring in the ventricles of the heart of the 'New Revolution'. But really it's all a matter of how to bring all modes and levels of liberation together and the key to such liberation is a consciousness of the subtle as well as the obvious destruction of personal reality wrought by private property-owning, *which disowns legitimate privacy*, and its attendant attitudes. The so-called permissive society, which graciously permits freer expression of sexuality and liberal social protest and promotes more humane (not human) conditions for prisoners and mental patients, is nothing more than a mystifying spectacle designed to perpetuate *a far deeper repression of ecstasy*, a repression of creative suffering and joy, of madness and the free assumption of risk even to death – in short the repression of revolution in each person and for all people.

To return finally to some other related issues, I am going to say this: frigidity is a way of trying to push open the door of the refrigerator; premature ejaculation is never a 'suitable case for treatment', it is simply a rather clumsy but urgent way of trying to say a passionate 'hello'. Both the female state of unpreparedness for orgasm and the male state of non-erection or premature, non-orgasmic coming indicate nothing more, beyond the obvious political conditioning that creeps into bed with all of us, than the necessity of touching, holding and exploring each other for a time that exceeds bourgeois time. And then also an initiatory help may be needed by either or both partners, sexual relating with one or two third persons of sufficient experience: the heterosexual person may need help from an experienced heterosexual or homosexual other, or the homosexual person *may* need help from either a homo- or heterosexual third person to achieve orgasm in the primary couple of whatever sex they are.

Then again there are 'perversions' to consider. So-called perversions are not sexual illnesses but rather tentative sexual solutions, socially isolated plunges into the still waters of love – but it's still about love. Because it's still about love it's never a 'psychopathological problem', only, perhaps, a profound problem of loneliness. There are no psychopathological problems and psychopathology must now be regarded as just about the most obscene word of all – precisely because of its non-recognition of love. It is a totally destructive, conservative, nosological public convenience dressed up as science. Certainly one has to demystify certain issues around, say, a 'rubber fetish-ism', or 'exhibitionism' or 'bestiality', but the answer is not to stop but carry *through it* to the fullest, joyful sexuality and life, when finally two people come together. One point to be clear about, however, is regarding 'sado-masochism'; a point that becomes very confusing for many people: sado-masochistic actions with the other cease to be acts that lead up to genital fulfilment at the exact moment when objective physical injury is inflicted on the other person – at that moment the act becomes totally asexual and non-orgasmic. But, in brief, 'perver-sions' only exist as evil aberrations in the sunken, unsee-ing eyes of the beholder, the 'normal citizen', who defines himself by his attitudes as nothing more than a boring curiosity – a freak for whom no shred of dignity remains after his prenatal dose of thalidomide of the spirit.

Non-orgasm and political reaction go hand in hand – we have to achieve their simultaneous abolition. One has only to look at the pathetic non-orgasmic faces of the bourgeois puppet 'leaders', the Hitlers, Nixons, etc. and all their mini-equivalents in present-day Europe whose only acts are the acts of the system that spewed them up as active non-realities. Bourgeois society is con-demned to government by eunuchs whose faces all bear the same 'Nixon Look'.*

For the sake of orgasm which is the secret centre of lib-eration we have to achieve a neat operation – we have to

* Just as it is possible physiognomically to assess the quality of a person's accumulated experience, the inscription of suffering on a face, so it is possible to form a clear impression of the dead-eyed orgasmic face and of orgasmic movement and speech. Non-orgasmic speech, for instance, never fits in with the talk or feelings of another, lacks tensioned discipline, exudes fear in its content, and is spas-modic, covertly brutal and compulsive and, above all, never creates a well-formed silence.

eliminate our poor poisoned brains by effecting a decapitation of ourselves that will at last lead us back to a lost life – and then forward.

We have to lose our heads to enter our bodies.

There is a time for minds, a time to leave our minds and a time to recover them.

5

What is Anti-Psychiatry?

When I introduced the term anti-psychiatry in a book published six years ago called *Psychiatry and Anti-Psychiatry*,* I had no idea how many innocent workers in the field of madness – on both sides of the supposed and actual fence between madmen and healers of madmen – would be caught up in a mythical and mystique-full web that was later generated around this apparently simple hyphenated word. Nor did I realize how many professionals would use it as some sort of identity tag. Some have clearly and correctly dissociated themselves from this onerous label, and with due respect for professional anonymity, I am grateful to them. Since, however, no one has adequately defined what anti-psychiatry is there seems to be nothing to associate oneself with or dissociate oneself from.

Anti-psychiatry for me was and is clearly susceptible to definition and, although hitherto I have only tried to show by actual examples what I mean by this concept, it is about time to list unequivocally the points of antagonistic contradiction that exist between this apparently negative entity and the patently extant and positive profession that is 'state-registered' as Clinical Psychiatry and which in

* David Cooper, *Psychiatry and Anti-Psychiatry*, Tavistock Publications, London, 1967.

England forms royal associations and colleges and so on, and which in other countries also, most obviously the two super-powers, is clearly part of a policing operation by the state to suppress difference, originality, vision and to deny the resolute refusal of certain people to be made less than human in any way. Clinical psychiatry, however, is only a small part of an extensive system of violence, of normalizing techniques that commence with the principal conformism-inducing instrument of the bourgeois state, the family, and run on through primary and secondary schooling and universities aiming to produce and then reproduce an endless assembly-line of indentical industrious creatures who all work for some Purpose which has long been lost sight of and which was never very visible in the first place anyhow.

Firstly we have to recognize the game structure of psychiatry; the carefully uncaring ways in which it leaves the healing tradition of medicine and becomes part of the state system of inducing conformism and reducing persons. A scientific tradition that moves through experience, diagnosis, prognosis and treatment becomes a micro-political operation of labelling and then systematically destroying by the psychiatric Cure. This Cure* is accomplished when the former person becomes an obedient robot moving around either in the chronic back wards of the psychiatric institution or moving without any more human sense in the outside society – like all the other non-people who bear a humanoid countenance and who retain no capacity to remember a long-forgotten world of dreams, images and spontaneous action. The bourgeois psychiatrist succeeds when his victim (patient) is reduced to nothing more

* Although lexicographically the meaning of cure includes care and attention, there is no etymological link between cure and care.

than the wretched, forsaken condition into which the psychiatrist himself has fallen.*

Anti-psychiatry tries to reverse the rules of the psychiatric game as a prelude to stopping such games. For example we may take the matter of 'diagnosis' and then consider what an anti-diagnosis might be. A girl I knew in a psychiatric institution had been diagnosed as schizophrenic because amongst other things she had the 'delusion' that she had changed into a long, vine-like, green plant that was growing every day towards the sun, and she expressed this by strange, slow, writhing movements of her body starting with movements of her feet and then ascending her body and finishing with her arms extended above her head. An anti-diagnosis here would be, not an objectifying label applied by an observer, but the girl's own central statement about what she felt herself to be together with her beautiful dance *as witnessed by the other*. *The need for a witness* is certainly one of the deepest human needs and one to which I shall return in this book. Only an extremely mystified person can need to be diagnosed, to have the 'security' of being definitely labelled, since diagnosis is a way of not witnessing, it is the way of objectification of the other as opposed to the intersubjectivity of witnessing. Certainly it might be important to arrive at an intelligibility of the experience of transformation into a plant and its curious choreography, but only in so far as this does not violate the present reality of her experience for which she needed a witness, not an interpretation. Also, certainly not tranquillizing drugs – those Abortifacients of the Spirit.

Another way of reversing the rules of the psychiatric

* There are some psychiatrists, however, working inside the system who are secretly anti-psychiatrists. They will know that my remarks do not apply to them.

game is by attacking the unidirectional role structure of psychiatrist versus patient and replacing it by a relationship of reciprocity. Reciprocity is impossible within the infantilizing, paternalistic structure of the psychiatric institution or in most psychotherapeutic situations where the structuring of the context precludes reciprocity. When groups of people live together in communes, however, other possibilities arise: in such a group some people may be 'professionals' and others 'patients' by exterior definition but at certain points these exterior roles may be reversed and the 'professional' may go into a disintegrative experience and be cared for by a 'patient'. This abolition of roles through reversal and then re-reversal works well when a certain homeostasis is achieved once the group has built up a strong enough solidarity and its own particular tradition as an anti-family.

Perhaps the most central characteristic of anti-psychiatry, however, is the recognition of the need for attentive non-interference aimed at *the opening up of experience rather than its closing down*. The condition for the possibility of this is being with the right other people, that is to say people who have sufficiently explored their own interiority and their own despair.

Lastly anti-psychiatry is political and is subversive by its very nature to the repressive bourgeois social order; not only because it validates certain forms of behaviour that are highly nonconformist, but also because it entails radical sexual liberation. What I have outlined above is subversive enough when it gets extensive enough, and talking to many students and young professionals in various countries has led me to believe that the existing psychiatric establishments will become totally discredited and unacceptable in the next two decades and they will not be replaced by institutionalized forms of anti-psychiatry which are impossible in principle since anti-psychiatry in its very nature must be involved in permanent revolution. Any worker in this field, the mad-sane one and the sane-mad one, is also committed to involvement to the maximum of his possibilities in the revolutionizing of the whole bourgeois society. In this sense anti-psychiatry, despite its formal negation, must be seen as highly positive.

The barricades are being built now.

*

Having said this much about what anti-psychiatry seems to me to be about, I am going to return to the point of consciousness at which its invention seemed necessary. When I worked as a psychiatrist in institutions in England I was obliged to attend meetings of the medical and lay administrations of those institutions. All the time I experienced a total sense of unreality about what those well-trained-to-heel curators or cremators of the soul talked about and believed they were doing – not out of any sort of malevolence nor out of any sort of latter-day saintliness but out of sheer mind-blinded, honest-to-goodness professionalism. If one were to speak to any of them alone there would always be a chance of some sort of recognition on their part that they were something more than their paraded collective *persona*; but this chance was always quickly lost in the terror of seeing themselves alone in the world as autonomous human beings without the totally abstract institutional backbone that sustained their personal flaccidity. Some of them supplemented this sort of non-existence (which, by its very nature of pretended being covering the nothing, could be so evidently destructive) by the further institution of 'individual' private practice – the last three words speak for themselves.

After a while I evaded this sort of infinitely earnest and

unsurpassably moronic non-meeting and spent the time being with the 'psychotic' victims of their deliberations. The latter, however battered by psychiatric cure, seemed somehow to survive in ways that were enlivening to me despite the prescribed progressive loss of vitality that they were undergoing. It was certainly vastly preferable to me than the blind-deaf-mute eunuchism of most of their professional guardians. It did not take much further experience of the most 'advanced' psychotherapeutic clinics in other countries to arrive at the same experiential conclusion.

In the psychiatric institution the keepers exercise their power against the kept by means of the social processes of admission (involving baptism by diagnosis or at least classification as 'dangerous to oneself' or 'dangerous to others') and subsequent rapid institutionalization so that continued detention, out-patient control or progressively easy re-admission may ensue. Mind-colonizing power is further exercised by treatment with drugs aimed at reducing experience and producing obedience, and which, when used massively and indiscriminately and often clearly punitively, may destroy bodies (as in chemical castration) as well as minds – as with electro-shock and psycho-surgery and with manipulative indoctrination in therapeutic groups and communities. The keepers in the hospital, who have concentrated in themselves a generally inculcated social fear, fear their own madness and deal with it not by experiencing it but by controlling the madness of the kept. Also, and this is much more destructive, they envy the madness of the inmates insofar as this signifies some sort of breakthrough or liberation that they prohibit themselves, therefore *the envied madness of the other has to be eliminated* – if not, the whole society might come to pieces, who knows? Of course there are many people working professionally in psychiatric institutions who honestly strive to understand madness and something of institutional violence, but if they try to act on their understanding, they rapidly go out on a limb where they are at the mercy of the frightened petty bureaucrats, medical and non-medical mind-police whose attitudes are a concentrate of the controllers of society outside the institution.

I think, therefore, that it might be useful, at the risk of repeating arguments that I put forward in similar phrasing in other parts of this book, and have done in previous books, to say some more about the relation between normality (and its paradoxes) and the different modes of madness.

'Primary socialization' in the family and subsequent 'secondary socialization' in the extra-familial society of school, university, trade union, profession and so on, induce a conformism that lies (in every sense of lying) in polar opposition to states of sanity and madness.* Sanity and madness meet at the opposite pole, the only difference being that the sane person unlike the mad person retains, with a bit of luck, sufficient of the normal strategies, *of the appearance not the fact of conformism*, to avoid invalidation, i.e. being made into an invalid or patient by the predators of the Normal World. The state of normality, at the other pole, represents the arrest or sclerosis of a person and at least the moronization if not the death of personal existence. This normalization process is founded on the desire for an equable, progressively convenienced, secure, 'happy' and easy life which is certainly some sort of death. Accordingly all signs of life, ecstatic intensities of

* I have written extensively about this particular point in *Psychiatry and Anti-Psychiatry*, Chapter 1, also in *The Death of the Family*, Chapter 1.

experience in joy which traverse the frontiers of despair and suffering, and orgasmic love, are prohibited.

To draw a profile of the Normal Man in the full glory of his unrecognized despair, we shall have to examine some of the structures of oppression and the suppression and repression of his experience. Oppression is more obvious but we have to carefully differentiate suppression and repression. In repression a secondary awareness acts on a primary awareness to make us aware of the primary awareness. In suppression a tertiary awareness acts on the secondary awareness to make us unaware that the secondary awareness is making us unaware of the primary awareness. To rid ourselves of reified constructs like repression it is a good cathartic exercise to use the truth-language of awareness. If it seems somewhat contorted it is because civilized life is contorted.

The actions involved in 'being a man', namely never being able to be 'child-like' ('good') as distinct from 'childish' ('bad'), being the strong, emotional support (though never showing feelings) for 'his' wife are obvious. Also obvious are the actions of 'being a woman' – being a man's property, being exhibited like prize cattle in beauty contests, her only place being the home. Less obvious is the nature of acts of liberating madness. These acts begin to destructure normality or the cancerous growth of incipient normality in the course of childhood and adolescence. These acts are ways of breaking through the blockage introduced by the continuing internal operation of primary and secondary socialization in the adult, and by new conformist pressures in the present.

The term madness is somewhat ambiguous and there are different modalities of it.

Firstly, there is madness as social stigmatization, the state of affairs produced by a planned series of social acts –

with varying degrees of awareness. A common example of this would be 'paranösogenesis': inauthentically functioning groups need a victim, who can in due course be dismissed as 'paranoid', to embody the negative aspects of everyone's feeling. Someone, for example, in a work group might become the object of envy of her or his colleagues, perhaps because he has a special insight into a basic flaw in their common project; this person is then victimized in various subtle ways for the sake of the group-unifying project and perhaps critical remarks about that person may be half-heard as someone else is leaving the room (hopefully to produce 'auditory hallucinations'). Finally the person, who has become progressively uncertain about his perceptions of persecution, is eliminated by being invalidated as paranoid and the group is left feeling justified and pleased with itself. The real conspiracy has been effectively concealed and a false conspiracy, the paranoid 'illness', forced into existence. Many forms of family 'schizogenesis', using double-binds, etc., function in the same way of course and the intelligibility of the so-called psychotic symptoms can be worked out. This is madness between inverted commas and it by no means implies that the person called mad has embarked on a significant inner voyage – although such a voyage *may* ensue.

Another madness is that of the inner voyage to which actual others may have only minimal relevance, although there may be a 'schizogenic trigger'. This is a voyage through the destructuring of alienated experience towards the restructuring of non-alienated experience. Here the difficult work of a therapeutic commune is not simply to eliminate schizogenetic factors in the person's life, including work on the person's family or network of significant others (neighbours, work-mates, etc.) but it is essentially the work of non-interference that I refer to elsewhere as the Taoist principle of *wu-wei*; this means in this context letting the mad person be, while at the same time always being available to him (as he in turn will be available to oneself at certain points in one's own voyage)*. This is where psychiatric treatment in any of its usual forms is a disastrous interference. Non-interference plus the availability of non-terrified persons is the central feature of anti-psychiatry. Examples of madness in this sense would include the madness of Gérard de Nerval, Antonin Artaud, Hölderlin and so on. But they had no one to 'be with'.

Thirdly, there is madness on the mass-social level. This third madness, unlike the first two, is clearly evil and I prefer to refer to it as *craziness* – craziness is the failed madness of the eknoid ('out of his mind'), totally conditioned Normal. The atrocities of imperialism, racism, sexism, ecocide and menticide are the crazy creations of officially normal minds. The overt or covert war of an imperialist power against a third-world nation is analogous† to the situation in a family where the one thing the family cannot tolerate is the assertion of *autonomy* on the part of one of its members so that a point is reached at which the

---

* The disruption of communion by communication of certain interpretations may happen even if the interpretation is not spoken – the fact that a person is mentally forming an interpretation of the other's behaviour never totally escapes the awareness of the other. In communion a person knows, often without, or in spite of, words, that the other is knowing him and that the other knows that the person knows that the other knows his knowing of him.

† There is an obvious danger in analogical argument from the micro- to the macro-political, but in the present context there is a clear unifying link: the panic-stricken need on the part of the holders of material and institutional power on both micro and macro levels to suppress the autonomous self-assertion of powerful people.

one who dares to assert the right to autonomy has to be invalidated. So, for instance, the people of Vietnam have to be invalidated and physically raped and eliminated in an insane passion to destroy the autonomous one in so far as the autonomous one embodies the freedom and responsible self-determination that the persecutor so fears and detests *in his own range of possibilities*. The same madness characterized the Nazi state where the ruling élite elaborated a delusional system in which they believed that the earth was hollow with superhuman beings beneath who guided the Nazi élite by strange cosmic influences; any 'otherness' that might assert itself had to be repressed, e.g. Jews, Gypsies, Slavs, psychiatric patients used as training material for the S.S.

Finally, the anti-psychiatrist is one who is prepared to take the risks involved in progressively and radically altering the manner in which he lives*. He must be prepared to give up the security devices of property (beyond the necessary minimum), exploitative money-games, and static, comfortable, family-like relationships as opposed to solidarity and comradeship with those who, with all the power of love and generosity are similarly opposed to the trivialization of experience which is the aim of bourgeois education and psychiatry. He must be prepared fully to enter his own madness, perhaps even to the point of social invalidation, since unless he does this he has no qualification. Anti-psychiatry is an urgently necessary part of the permanent revolution, or it is nothing.

I have said that the sane person retains sufficient of the

* A number of people are labelled anti-psychiatrists or cash in on labelling themselves thus while in fact practising quite conventional psychiatry and psycho-therapy with the usual power and money orientation. The prevailing romanticization of madness (which soft-pedals the central *suffering* of madness) makes this an easy number.

strategies of the normal state to escape being invalidated as mad, but sanity is a dangerous way to be since the very tactics of survival are in fact the very means by which we progressively destroy ourselves. Small wonder that the mood of anti-psychiatry must be one of compassionate anger.

If I sound angry in what I have said above, the answer is that I am furious.

Dare you not be?

6

Who Does the Analyst Pay?
A Glance at the Fraud Squad

Shame is a revolutionary sentiment too
Karl Marx

The original Vienna sausage should be squeezed between bread. Its historical fate is to be squeezed *by* bread – just plain bread without caraway seeds or a piquant mustard that would produce a true imperialist hot-dog.

Freud was the original *maître de cuisine* and the original recipe was a proposed solution to the *implicit* questions: 'how can we understand to the greatest possible extent the complex articulation of another person's life, and communicate that understanding to the other in such a way that he may transform his life in the direction of an unspecified but at least suggested goal of adjustment to an unfortunate but actual social reality?' And 'how can we (the doctors) do this in an economically realistic way that does not threaten our socially defined normalcy and capacity to cope?'

In the development of psychoanalysis the answer to this latter question was found in the analysis of 'defence' structures and 'resistance'. Analysis along these lines, massively conditioned by the context in which central-European intellectuals lived in the early part of this century, provided a remarkable and temporarily impregnable defence of the analyst's role as the trustworthy person who understands objectively, who fully knows, by virtue of his training, his own feelings about himself and therefore about his feelings about you and ultimately your feelings about yourself; you who will be there in his appointed place at his appointed time, at his appointed fee, for *you* – or perhaps for your appointed disappointment.*

In the analytic situation disappointment has several meanings. One sense of disappointment is the necessary disillusionment that follows the realization that the analyst is not God, the omnipotent manipulator of our various destinies. Only later may one be able to be grateful for the stupid analyst who has the modesty to strive for attentiveness and to refrain from interfering.

Another sense of disappointment, however, and one that can never be analysed away, comes from the recognition of non-reciprocity in the analytic 'relationship', a recognition of the impossibility of mutual recognition – unless one reduces mutual recognition into some vague feeling of understanding and being understood.

The analyst's recognition or re-knowing of himself can never be an accomplishment prior to a particular analytic relationship since that would aprioristically deny the possibility of relationship. Every bit of re-knowing of oneself, of relating to another from the re-traced origins of one's present self, must be newly forged in each new relationship that is significant in the sense of being a

* As in legal marriage the psychoanalytic relation between people has the dice heavily loaded against it ever becoming an authentic relationship from the start – because of the introduction of the alienating and destructive factor of money (Hegel's 'the life of what is dead moving inside itself'), the law or professional contract, and property.

relating *from* our origins, *through* the present *towards* what is ultimately a totally unconditioned future.

Freedom is bivalent in so far as it operates through (on the way through) conditioning (as the marxist 'recognition of necessity') but also as what is beyond this conditioning. 'Beyond' here implies a non-decadent spirituality as expressed in the concluding paragraph of Jeremias Gotthelf's book *The Black Spider* (1842)* which may be paraphrased as the fair sharing of the power of being between the sinister and the luminous forces in the world; god is the standing invitation to us to upset the balance either way by the very next act that each and any of us may carry out†. In any case there is no contradiction between these notions of freedom. Both proceed carrying their heads high in the same direction.

We have to inquire, I believe, into the possibilities that the person 'being analysed' has of reaffirming his self-perceptions, after due examination of these perceptions in the context of the aspiring relationship. Instead of comforting abdication to the analyst's perceiving – a sweet, warm, passive, penny-in-the-slot acquiescence – perhaps the person can after all stick to his guns, whatever the risks of being socially shot down. In conventional psychoanalysis the analysand becomes the non-human bull's eye in a target practice that rehearses the risks of waiting for the last-minute reprieve when humanly facing the really potent bullets of the firing-squads of the minions of bourgeois society. What I have called conventional psychoanalysis seems to me to be spectacularly unuseful

---

* Translated, Calderbooks, 1958.

† This 'very next act' is not unconditional but one *beyond conditioning*, in the sense that there is a massive undifferentiated, unarticulated realization, beyond words, of the totality of one's conditioning from which a free act issues.

in avoiding the fate of falling back into the mass grave in which most people in our society, 'riddled' in every sense, are already merely waiting to die.

A woman, eighteen years old, whom I was to meet and talk with some ten years later, leaves her city in the north of Argentina, a city where the commercial enterprises of her family prosper, a city where the despoliation of the sugar-producing land and the dispossession of the poor goes on by virtue of the elbow-grease that has no elbow of the successive impotent puppet régimes of generals who rule from the south, paid off by imperialist money. Her family is an opaque inky substance to her and as she cannot blot it up she decides simply to leave it. So she goes to Buenos Aires, her one-shot-loading rifle replete with a simple realization: her family, Jewish emigrants to the third world from central Europe, had somehow got things wrong and that was why she was in despair. She wasn't quite sure how much the getting wrong was their 'fault' or how much was due to the mere fact of her presence in their world. Maybe she should not have been born into their world or just not have been born. But she had been and she went along to her first analyst, a woman, with the naïve question – 'It's all a problem in our family – what can I do about it? . . . it's like this . . .'

First interruption by analyst, repeated through all calculable permutations to that point of infinity that remains finally in the world: 'You are not talking to me about your family in city X, you are trying to tell me something about a version you have inside yourself about your father and mother up there, and your brother and sister up there, but you must understand that I don't know those people up there, I can only know about those things inside you that you will tell me about. Then we will work and I may help you.'

WOMAN: 'But why can't you know them? They are really there in city X and there's a telephone next to you. Can't you call them and make sure that they really are there because I'm beginning to be uncertain if they really are now?'

ANALYST: 'How can I know everything in the world as you seem to demand? What we have to know is what goes on here, now. We have to know what goes on inside you here because you can only see me now through that confusion inside yourself.'

WOMAN: 'But it's true. My mother was sick all the time, she was very depressed or angry or something . . . she used to hit me so often and so hard whenever my father went out and I didn't know what was wrong with me. He never stopped her, my father, but he knew what would happen when he went to work . . . so when he went to work I went to my grandparents . . . my mother's mother and her husband. Grandmama used to talk such a lot that she got cancer of the voice box in the end and died of it. Grandpapa was deaf for years before that and when she was dying on her bed she asked him to kiss her for the last time before she went and all he could say was "what . . . what . . . can you speak louder . . . ?" and before she died she whispered through her cancer "you've never loved me?" He miraculously got his hearing back after that but that's not the point. The point is that they must have been like my parents . . . speaking and not being heard, dying alone, because they have to live alone, my mother's needing me to look after her – demanding it and knowing it was impossible, I mean it all seems to have happened like that, time after time after time.

'It all *happened*. They *are* there!'

ANALYST: 'Well, it may have happened something like that but is that really the point now? It seems that you are afraid that one bit of me will beat you as you say your mother did and that the other bit of me will fail to protect you as you feel your father failed you. Perhaps you feel to be all bad because you are unable to bring your good experiences here because you fear that this evil person here, which is how you seem to see me, will destroy the good things stored inside you as you always feared your parents would. And then again you fear that I must be treacherous like those bits of your mother that you let yourself remember, turning a blind eye like your father, not listening like your grandmother who died of speaking too much, not hearing like grandpapa. You are putting all those bad bits that cause you so much pain inside yourself into me.'

WOMAN: 'But they *are* like that. *They* are there ... *there*, not inside me or you. I feel I must be mad.'

ANALYST: 'Well why do you think you are here? Isn't it a step forward to realize that you need help ... help in dealing with all those difficulties you have inside yourself?'

WOMAN: 'Thank you. I suppose now I know I am mad at least. When do you want me to come again?'

ANALYST: 'Your next appointment is tomorrow at twelve.'

And so on for five years. She lives a thousand miles away from her parents but the parents 'inside her' seem to remain a problem and when her remote but actual parents are nice to her the parents inside her get more and more intractable in their unobservable but demanding presence. When she realizes that her analyst is too much like this too she decides to change analyst at a point when she is finishing her degree course in psychology and starting to 'see' 'patients' too.

After two years with her second analyst she found herself in the same impasse in which she had lost herself in the previous analytic non-meeting. But there were differences. She was short of money for the analysis, which, together with professional supervision of her work as a therapist, cost her more than it cost her to live and she was trying to be financially independent. Her mother knew this and telephoned her analyst when she knew that 'her girl' would be in session. The brief telephone conversation as overheard by the girl amounted to the analyst's collusive confirmation of the mother's view that she was a really fine girl (implied: well brought-up, to be proud of) but still needed some important work to be done on her problems. So the mother obtained instant 'absolution', absolution since she felt that the fact that her daughter was seeing an analyst implied something wrong, in an almost legalistic, criminal sense, or crazy, which was about the same thing. So mother agreed to send her daughter a monthly cheque made out to the analyst to be delivered by her daughter to the analyst. The girl felt confusedly betrayed by these machinations; confusedly because she had internally and externally pledged herself to wholeheartedly trust the analyst – and now what had happened? But there was always the possibility that she really was 'paranoid' and, despite being a 'fine girl', she felt pretty mad, or 'psychotic', as she had been taught to see 'her patients'. Psychotic in some subtle Kleinian sense, no doubt, but at the same time mad enough in a socially defined way to feel that her institutionalized day-to-day working life was in danger of invalidation and that she might really become an objective psychiatric invalid in some more or less benign/malevolent bin.

So she went around to see various of her friends, sometimes staying overnight with them and finding some sustaining support because at least some of her friends were going through the same sort of thing and, without talk being necessary, they somehow seemed to understand even if they did not, any more than she, know what they seemed to understand. One thing that she really did know was that with one of her 'patients' she would have handled that telephone call differently. She would have said that she would discuss the fact of the phone call with the 'patient' and, if the patient agreed, would consider a joint meeting with mother, patient and herself – certainly not a meeting between mother and analyst that excluded the patient. Admittedly the handling of the telephone call was an exceptionally bad move on the analyst's part and by no means common in analysis but the general point about the exclusion or the distorted inclusion of reality outside the analytic situation holds.

It was when her first analyst finally did meet the mother alone that she decided after two years to make a fresh start with someone who had the reputation of being one of the best training analysts in the city. Surely he would be above such external manipulations of her situation; she would sacrifice almost any material comfort to pay his fees herself, and surely he at last would be the person who could confirm the reality of her view of the absurd persecutory things that had been and still were going on in her family.

But what happened?

An expensive nothing – so she found a fourth who might at last find her too.

There are good analysts but they have to be searched for very hard – a major part of the analytic work is finding a non-neutral analyst *who is on the same side as oneself*.

'Being on the same side' moves pyschoanalysis into politics. In the case of the Argentinian girl no room was allowed for her parents' personal reality actually in the north of the country and their *present* impingment on her life, their social and political conditioning in Europe and then South America. I have met so many examples of this blindness to the most obvious realities over the years (people whom I have seen after they have previously been in psychoanalysis in various countries), that I feel that there are now very few psychoanalysts anywhere who can help people while working in the old practical and ideological context. There are a few worthy triers left but if there is going to be any sort of revolution in and then out of psychoanalysis, it will be achieved by the 'patients' who, refusing to accept the evasive response that their political consciousness is an intellectual defence against 'deeper problems', insist on their total reality, not by psychoanalysts* – because the doctors *don't know*. *Psychoanalysis is a nuclear family ideology. Demystifying this dehumanizing institution entails the elucidation of a new political possibility*. Psychoanalysis as it is taught (the training) and practised in the conventional schools, by virtue of its implicit conformist values, becomes yet another agency in the employ of the endlessly devious, repressive and repressively 'tolerant' bourgeois system. A sort of CIA of the individual psyche.

The dependence on external defences such as time-and-money regulation of meeting is a presently necessary one for many psychoanalysts who may do very good work with the very few people they see. The movement into the macro-political is, however, now most urgent. Some do good work in the intermediary area of couples, families and networks – but the further step in the 'anonymous'

* For the sake of clarity I should remind some readers that here I am referring to trained psychoanalysts, or at least therapists who have undergone therapy themselves, and not pychiatrists, who, in their training, are not expected to have any *personal* experience of analysis or therapy although some in fact choose to.

collectivity of several hundred is much more difficult and cannot easily be made single-handed. This is why the old psychoanalytic associations in Europe and elsewhere are rapidly disintegrating and politically conscious young workers in the field of therapy are forming their own collectives and are living in situations where the therapeutic process, though disciplined, is natural and mutual between everyone.

What has to be done is penetrate the soft area of the system – that relatively small sector of all the people who can most significantly turn others on. This is way beyond any sort of professionalism and devolves onto writing, forming work groups with 'significant new ones', and commune formation, and is the most perilous journey for anyone who engages on it as it involves maximal self-exposure with minimal external defences against being swallowed up and against the formidable, fearful forces of envy and jealousy of one's personal relationships by those who have been led to believe that they may not express any creativity of their own. Or again, from third-world experiences I have had, there are the risks of arbitrary and violent police and para-police intervention. This has happened recently in Europe too, for example, the suppression and imprisonment of anti-psychiatric workers in the Heidelberg *Sozialistisches Patientenkollectiv*.

All relationships are therapy or they are violence. If one person in confusion seeks another person, in whose experience she or he trusts, a disciplined 'one-way' relationship for a while may be necessary – but on the way to free mutuality of relating.

Therapy in the only possible remaining sense begins when we stop trying to therapeutize or educate the people out of their germinal sense of reality and start opening ourselves to the changes that they will show us that we, and they, have to make. The 'us' and the 'them' will then be seen to be one. The infinitely divisive system of people who love but seem intent upon their destruction, and those who destroy while seeming intent on loving, will finally be broken down by a humility that works its way, using shame, through the entrails of a false pride in the direction of an ultimately triumphant and truly proud unity of the people. Thus will we become what we all are anyhow.

What is true of psychoanalytic therapy is also true for some of the new 'alternative therapies', which manifest an extraordinary manic flight towards power that no longer limits itself to (considerable) money but extends to control of minds and the invasion of areas of necessary sexual privacy, e.g. the 'touching-and-holding' salvationism, and undisciplined, essentially authoritarian non-encounter. Perhaps words like 'growth', 'development', 'force' and 'energy' should be removed from the market. Like educational 'knowledge commodities', therapeutic commodities are aimed at the incorporation of the recipient into the greed system of society.

The changes I would propose in therapy, now inextricably interwoven with education and the extension of political awareness in the broadest sense, put the therapist out in the world – and out in the world at risk.

But if we are not prepared to risk our minds and lives, we shall lose them anyhow.

Psychiatric symptoms can be seen with startling clarity as one form of defiance against the social lie. They are protest, though protest with contradictions built in. *Telling the truth*, in one way or another, is the commonest symptom of mental illness and the commonest reason for the invalidation of patients. Politically real therapy, as opposed to psychoanalysis as a survival kit for the normal world, exposes the contradictions and this amplifies the protest and facilitates the fuller emergence of the (often disguised) truth – the truth that would erase every lying word of the proprietary society. The contradiction to be dealt with is: that to maintain one's personal truthfulness, one has to learn how to lie to the agents of the proprietors on the way to the establishment of a general social truth.

7

Strategies for Defeat – Envy and Jealousy

I am going to examine the need to destroy envied persons in one mode of invalidation or another. This is one form of a more general political operation in which a micro-political scene mediates the macro-political need to create collectivities of invalidated persons of various categories so that the particular society is reassured of its essential rightness. This seems historically to be a need specific to property-owning societies and the reason seems to me to be that if the society can *own* certain people in such a way that it can either expel them to its limits or relegate them to an inferior status – that is *disown* them – then it can *own* everyone else as property. The ruling class in any society thus creates the state as a quasi-organism with certain needs. Thus the persecution of women, the 'racially inferior', the 'sexually deviant', lunatics, children, the religiously and ideologically different, and so on – all to satisfy this non-existent monster. It is curious how potent the non-existent can be if one believes in it hard enough.

Envy is a hatred* at the very source of one's life – because something, that the other supposedly had, was missing from oneself from the beginning. There are far more archaic frustrations in a person's life than the re-

* I prefer to talk of modalities of hatred rather than 'hatred' as such. The deepest of these modalities is envy.

peated no-breast experience – the fact that the baby wants the breast even when the baby's body does not biologically need it – a process culminating in weaning; and the sense of frustration that goes along with the mere so-called hallucinated breast. Though these frustrations are awarenesses of lack essential for 'development' they are filled with hatred because of the postulated other who has or is the continual good breast. Going back further, there is the rupture of the intact placental circulation at birth along with the prior emptying of the baby's ideal symbiotic medium, the amniotic fluid. The sole intelligibility of the baby's howl at birth is not to expand the lungs. The whole phenomenology* of birth is that of pain – of being cast into the world as a separate human entity. Before that one was a separate human entity (e.g. the doctor's dilemma: the mother's life or the baby's) but one was not cast out into the world – there was a safe enough symbiosis. Transformations of these experiences run on through the rest of our lives – only losing force as we gain in lucidity. For example there is the umbilical cord of the institutional matrix (mother substance); how many institutionalized men die on retirement when and because that link is broken? Only a lucidity made possible by a mass social change could save them.†

Prior to all this by nine months there is an earlier threat

* By 'phenomenology' I mean the study or examination of experience of experience unmediated by concepts or preconceptions. *Afterwards*, as many concepts as one needs. This non-appropriative experience of (one's own or another's) experience is opposed to the absurd appropriative projects of *having* the other's experience or re-owning one's already owned experience.

† In proprietary society an increase in leisure time can only destroy people in various ways because of the severance of the un-ligatured, institutional umbilical cord. The only more sinister thing

of the rupture of a primitive unity. There must be a phenomenology of the unfertilized ovum. Experience, now deeply buried, from the inside of the ovum. I know I am asking you to take experience in a very wide sense (and this is not all yet) but I believe we cannot arrive at a full intelligibility of our adult human life structures and especially the structures of madness (which very much involve ovarian experience) unless we do. As we know, at conception the ovum was 'split' (in the sense of the disturbance of a unity) by the spermatozoon, initiating a whole series of splits. The ovum in the mother 'becomes afraid' at the disintegrative entry of the spermatozoon: the earliest unity is broken and the dreaded incompleteness of separate being commences.

I believe further that there is a pre-conception, non-union experience. I do not expect all readers to go along with the idea of reincarnation (certainly not as usually stated) but it may explain a great deal that would otherwise be senseless – especially 'pure', non-intelligible madness, that is an inner journey initiated without significant micro-social schizogenesis. A separation occurs after death, before birth (as rebirth), and has been expressed as the non-union with the pure light of the Void.* Here envy refers to the actualized possibility, to those who did achieve such liberation from earthliness, into final union.

A special issue which we should examine is the personal

---

is the perpetuation of institutional dependence by institution-provided re-creational (!) facilities. It is not a matter of first envying and then hating the other because one envies him, but rather, in confronting the other, there is a realization of lack in oneself that is *immediately* filled with hatred.

* See *The Tibetan Book of the Dead*, ed. Evans-Wentz, in many different editions.

political one of *self-envy*. Although envy is classically a two-person situation in which the second person – the envier – may be replicated to form group envy of the first person, it may assume a monadic form – the split monad. There may be bits of oneself that one envies, hates and attempts to destroy. There may, for instance, be beautiful, internal creations of united sanity and madness that one is impelled to destroy by a 'bad' craziness – that is a craziness in which self-invalidation reinforces and is then reinforced by social invalidation.* Apart from behaviour that gets one labelled psychotic (in any form), these aspects of self may also be destroyed by heroin, alcohol, etc., or more simply and far more usually by living a normal life, that is, a crippled, visionless, arthropodan life that is forever safe from any dangerous liberation. I have said that self-envy is a personal political issue and it is in fact one of a reactionary series of acts that reinforces both the ethos and the power of the ruling class at every turn. It is essentially the acting into the world of an illusion – the illusionary, impossible division of a 'self' into hating and hated 'bits'. I have described earlier in this volume the absurdity of any notion of substantial self, so that 'bits of self' are absurd at a second remove. Treating oneself as another is originally a defence (in the sense that at least one of one's selves may escape in an extreme situation) but this defensive self-division can lead to defeat when it becomes the basis for self-envy.

Envy is a real and effective mode of acting in the world, however disastrous, but it involves a mystification. The central mystification involved in envying is the covering-up of the destruction by a thin tegument of love and concern.

* As distinct from madness that is purely socially ordained without significant self-invalidation, and madness that is pure, indestructible, autonomous poetry.

This is the case with two-person or group envy and with self-envy. One can destroy one's self or another with all the appearance of profound cosmic compassion. This compassion radiates out to everywhere except where the relevant people are. Further, situations arise according to the homeostatic law of the group, the law according to which one or more persons, regarded as deviant from the group objective, have to be offered up as sacrifices to maintain the integrity of the group that is a source of illusory strength to the other group members. These situations include for example that in which, if the invalidated envied person gets better, at least one other member of the group breaks down in one form or another – very much like the so-called 'marital see-saw'. The envied person in a group may of course also be a self-envying person and then the group rigidifies and there is no chance of another breaking down to release the self-victimizing victim. Ultimately such a group will disperse – at least unless there is some almost awe-inspiring change in the central personage.

In an earlier book* I described an ecstatic experience of cosmic compassion which I had. The compassion was and is real enough but it also masked a negative experience of self-envy that I was having, which resulted in a series of self-destructive moves over a period of several years. These moves involved amongst other things the wrong mode of entry into and conduct of relationships. Fortunately for the others at the end of these relationships I got worse and they usually appeared to become stronger. That it took some years for me to work through the self-envy problematic (envy of creating by writing and of informal therapeutic functioning in non-central but important relationships) is not surprising. More usually it never hap-

* *The Death of the Family*, p. 42.

pens, since compounded states of envy by or of others and self-envy constitute the most intractable micro-political problematic of all. We have to be absolutely lucid about these operations of envy in a commune. Otherwise there is always a disastrous group dispersion. That has been my experience in more than one commune situation that I have observed.

Previously* I have dealt with the subject of jealousy in terms of the pain of jealousy being an enforced separateness as distinct from elected autonomy. If, of a couple A and B, B has a relationship with person C then A is placed in a position of separate being, a situation of freedom which can be developed as either a good aloneness (autonomy) or a deprived loneliness (mere separateness). This is much more painful than A's reflections (in the male case) on his virility or confusion about the acting out of his passive homosexual wishes.

Envy essentially is the desire to *be* the other while jealousy is the desire to *have* the other.

Jealousy thus seems to be essentially a polyadic situation involving three persons, unlike envy which is two-person or one-person. Things are not so simple, however, because one discovers also a monadic jealousy – the classical three persons may be condensed into one person. One may be jealous of one's own potency – and I do not mean simply sexual potency but also potency for acquiring metaphorical food (i.e. any sort of 'good thing' that one might 'take in'). Both sex and food equal property in this system.

This all involves complex splits. For example, in making love one may feel split off from one's own sexuality so that it is as if some vague third person, one's self made other, were making love to one's partner and one may

* 'The Topography of Love', *The Death of the Family*.

have the illusion that one's partner is betraying one. One may secretly estimate one's potency so highly, while overtly to one's self underestimating it, that the potency of the imaginary third may seem much greater than one's own. This is where envy overlaps jealousy because one envies the potency of the imaginary third, in the sense of wanting to become 'him', i.e. to become one's self more fully. The important thing is that this illusory triadic scene leaves one feeling in the same painful situation of enforced separateness as the real triadic situation does.

Similarly, in masturbation one may be the one left out while one 'internal' other makes love with another internal other. It is clear that this can be the most mystifying jealousy situation of all – the polyadic monad. A great deal of so-called 'masturbation guilt' is really feeling remorse about the 'reasonless' jealous hatred involved in the machinations of the purely internal triad. The triad may even assume the nature of a primal scene drama. One's self[1] witnessing one's self[2] being fucked by one's self.

Three-person jealousy may be vastly complicated by the simultaneous working of one-person jealousy, and much useful therapeutic clearance work can be done by eliminating the one-person jealousy, so that one is left with the objective triadic situation. The 'vibrations' of one-person jealousy operating in person A in a couple A-B may be picked up by the partner in a couple who then proceeds to provoke a triadic jealousy scene involving C in a couple B-C; the impulse is to relieve anxiety by making concrete something which is mystifyingly present but not apparent. There are other self-defeating scenes, complicated or not by self-jealousy, that elude 'classical' jealousy.

One common three-person scene is where person A is 'ill' in the sense of being 'out of action' or not being able to know much of what goes on, for whatever reason. Person C then attempts to seduce A's partner B, in the belief that the violence of jealousy might be avoided while at the same time person C would feel that he had been triumphant and sexually superior (as a potent presence) to the 'absent' A. This is a dangerous form of self-mystification on C's part that B may compound by colluding with it. It is quite opposite to any form of sexual feedom. It is similar to the compulsive unfree way that widows and widowers are sometimes pursued.

Again, there is the three-person situation that would enact the primal scene. Firstly, let me say that there is never any 'primal scene trauma' in the conventional sense. The only 'trauma'* happens when the parents frighten the child with their conditioned fear of being observed while making love. If the parents are free of this fear they do not frighten the child and there is no trauma. When the primal scene is re-enacted between three adults the situation is something like this, say: an older man is in bed with a woman; a younger man who is closely attached to the older man gets into bed, too, permission being taken for granted, and makes love somewhat furtively with the woman; he is temporarily relieved but his phantasy was that, in making love with the woman, he was being passively penetrated by the older man – this was the closest he could get to living out his passive homosexual wishes. But the illusion runs its course and when the illusion is no longer possible the outcome for the young man is breakdown in some form – the outcome

* By trauma I mean simply any radically self-altering experience by which one's autonomy is reduced – either enforced by the other(s) or through some collusion with the other(s).

of the 'breakdown' may be good (breakthrough) or bad according to the quality of the relationship between the three people (capacity for insightful non-collusion) or the intervention of a fourth person who understands what is going on. Such has been my experience on a number of occasions in communal living. Communes are a dangerous business but our times are desperate and, once again, we have to take certain risks in order to create a trust that obviates strategies for defeat – and ultimately strategies in general.

In the case of both envy and jealousy, the challenge is for us to accept our autonomy and our essential aloneness in struggle. Solidarity is then created on the basis of the courageous assumption of a good aloneness.

To accept our autonomy is to become politically real.

8

The Inner is the Outer

Those apparently indispensable verbal conveniences, the inner and the outer, and their consequent psychoanalytic conceptualizations, introjection and projection, have finally to be dispensed with. Firstly, because they are merely linguistic conveniences lacking any ulterior reality. Secondly, because they are intellectual constructs, derived from a narrow physical scientific conception of space, that are imposed on experience and distort experience; although it is true that skilful psychoanalysts use language in the 'talking cure' in a way that seems to avoid these concepts, they in fact remain implicit in the thinking behind such language. Thirdly, because they are an intrinsic part of a whole system involving such notions as 'the self' and 'the unconscious' – that is, one mode of reflection on experience rather than the direct encounter of experience with experience – an immense distance being thus imposed between the experience of one person and that of another in their free interplay.

I admit however, to using constructs such as internalization and externalization in this book but this is the only way I could find, as a temporary expedient, to get a less conventional way of thinking things out to meet with a more conventional, and now antiquated, way. The antiquated way is oppositional and anti-dialectical.

Everything in experience has to be put inside or outside certain selves. This convenient model breaks down when the specific nothingness of the self is realized – nothing can contain nothing, much less an 'internal object'. There is nothing left of the self but its specificity which is defined by specific experiential acts which are all in the world. But the differences implied by inner-outer language can be experienced as very real (that is, they *happen* in the sense of being acted into existence); for example, the difference between torturer and tortured. The interdependence of torturer and tortured demonstrates the unitary character of being: one cannot exist without the other, but the otherness is the index to change within the unity. My earlier account in this book of experience as non-spatio-temporal direction, and action on experience as deflection of experience, will, I hope, help get rid of the particular meta-level of thinking in terms of self, conscious and unconscious self and hence notions of 'projection' and 'introjection'. Projection is pure, though deformed, action in the world and so is introjection. Projection is not an act 'in' someone that passes out into the world and then ends up 'in' or 'on' someone else. Projection falsely modifies the experienced and acted-on world, and introjection falsely modifies the apparent 'actor' in the world. *All is out in the world – there is no reality behind the manifestations of reality, but although I say all is outside, all is also inside the outside.* It is true that there is a personalizing factor but this factor is defined by directions as I have described them. The question is why the differentiation of the inner and outer has arisen. The answer is that it is a way, a necessarily false one, of understanding human experience from a point remote from that experience. It has nothing to do with the unitary act of experience experiencing itself – that is non-mediated experience. The remoteness is convenient, since closer touching of experience by experience induces a terror of the nothing that is where the substantial centre of the experiencing self is supposed to be.

It may be necessary to give some examples: A man fears his homosexual wishes and fears that another man wishes to rape him anally. Here the man deflects his wish into the more or less experienced wish of the other man. Certainly the 'projecting' man in question effects this deflection of experience – into the supposed though possibly actual experience of the other. But in any case it is a matter of pure action in the world. The illusion of interiority. All action and acted-upon experience happens out in the world where action after all belongs. The same is the case with 'introjection'. Say one introjects one's mother or an aspect of one's mother. This means nothing more than that one acts like one's mother or aspects of one's mother in the world. This purity of experience, acted-upon experience and action achieves a unitary plenum of existence.

Reductive interpretations of projection are a way of getting the person to conform with the normal, conventional world but some sort of interpretative attitude is present in most cultures. Whether the interpretation be psychoanalytically explicit or culturally implicit is a matter of indifference. The social effect of understanding actions in terms of projection is the same. Once again the world is all that is inside the outside. Similarly, interpretation of introjection that overlooks its sole reality as action in the world lacks the essential dimension of externality in opposing inner to outer: no introject has meaning apart from its expression in the world. The world, that is inside the outside, once again is all that matters.

The therapeutic implications of this way of thinking

things out are immense. Instead of reflecting on the experience of the other and then commenting from the base of one's reflections, one has a situation in which experience *meets* experience and deflected experience; 'projection' and 'introjection' are returned to the point from which directions were misdirected – not necessarily by verbal messages. This may entail accepting projections without interpretation, since this apparent quietism may effect the redirection (not into or out of anything) much more effectively than any verbal interpretation. The emphasis is on comprehension without the compulsive expression of one's comprehension. By definition I can give no examples of this attitude – one either 'has it' or does not.* The disciplined restraint implied by this mode of being with the other is, to say the least, considerable. There is no room left for the compulsive interpreter. Such a compulsion is as severe as any hard-drug addiction and can only be broken by a lengthy training, or rather untraining or anti-training. Just as hard drugs are a disguised method of control, destructive control, so is compulsive interpretation. A successful de-controlling operation is required, along with the acquisition of a true personal discipline.

One version of projection is like turning a non-existent coat inside out so that the inner lining of oneself shows itself to the world. Thus, what is understood by 'projection' is a state of extreme vulnerability, a form of nakedness or exposure. Certainly it is a 'defence' against 'greater dangers' (I have to use inverted commas to express sufficient irony about the use of these terms that have been conventionalized out of any original sense). The greater dangers are the realization of the presence of

* One can learn much about this attitude, however, by *being with* someone who 'has it'.

the projected characteristic in oneself. The vulnerability of projection resides in the fact that the language that expresses it cannot be literal – otherwise the 'game' would be given away. The language has to be metaphorical because the truth would be totally unacceptable socially, and metaphor exposes one to the danger of being regarded as a psychotic person.

I should point out here that I am talking about 'projection' in the case of individual persons. If the ruling class *en masse* resorts to projective systems it can get away with it for a while, to the immense cost of everyone else.

The central point I want to make is that, far from being pure error, what has been called projection is a groping deflected way of arriving at a new and difficult truth. Projection is human experimentation that takes a risk. This emphasizes my point about accepting projections – not only does one have to accept projections but one might have to confirm the true centre of projections.

Much is entailed in this transvaluation of psychoanalytic values. It certainly entails a radical break with all those elements of the psychoanalytic process that induce conformism. I say 'process' because as a rule it is a process and not a mode of action on experience. The free interchange of experience breaks all the rules of the psychological game, and that seems to be dangerous enough both ways. But unless one takes this risk nothing of any import happens – nothing except the tricky induction of a due conformism.

Introjects are not quasi-substantial lumps of otherness in the middle of some supposed self. They are directions, in my previous sense of direction, that are powerfully redirected back towards where they came from after a moment of contact with their target. For example the good breast or its substitute are experienced and then there is a powerful return towards the one who experiences, the source, the non-substantial initiation of direction. The power is in the very nature of the direction. The determinant of the degree of power lies in the target or mode of termination of the direction. The good breast may be more powerful than any other aspect of the other – or it may be less powerful. Personal liberty, to relapse into the old language, depends on the powerful expulsion of the introject – a power that is greater than that of the process of introjection. After induction into the bourgeois family way of living, the power that generates liberty becomes increasingly difficult to achieve.

I have said that in principle nothing can be said about a compulsion-free analytic procedure of responding to experience by experience, but perhaps this is not quite true. At least in a negative sense there are ways of describing the procedure. For the therapist it is a matter of resolutely refusing to be *the target* of 'projections'. This certainly does not mean any non-acceptance of the other person's statements but it does mean an end to any inviting collusion with the other. Such collusions are contrived only too readily by both parties since there is nothing more secure and non-changing than a collusive symbiosis. It takes a lengthy process of intimidation, over years or centuries, for an oppressed race to fall into a collusion with its oppressors. What has to be achieved is the difficult work of refusing to be altered by the deflected directions of the other. In micro-political but never in macro-political terms:

Stand still and let it happen around you.

Don't take into yourself anything you don't need.

This, however, is a counsel of perfection, since the conditioning of any person brought up in a typical bourgeois nuclear family makes the urge to symbiose blindly with the family, and then later to involve others in similar symbioses, almost irresistible. The only answer is to see the essential identity of the 'inner' and the 'outer' family and to confront this identity with a fully justified counter-violence.

I am writing about a trap into which even the most experienced people repeatedly fall. After the fall there develops a hard lastingness. The best way out of the trap is never to fall into it. Falling into the trap is based on the convenient illusion of quasi-substantial selves that have a sort of semi-permeable membrane through which some 'objects' selectively pass both ways.

The age of this lying metaphor has been passed.

Perhaps now we have to begin to talk about what you do to me and I do to you.

9

Life Re-Lived

In 1916 Freud wrote of regression as a characteristic of 'psycho-neurotic conditions' each of which 'retraces the stages of its evolution', and in 1920 he wrote of regression as a 'reversion from a higher to a lower stage of development in general'. In 1912 he had posited the occurrence or non-occurrence of regression as contingent upon two factors: 'fixation' and 'frustration'. This view of regression as failure has to be radically overturned.* Certainly regression is discrepant with 'social reality', *but then one must consider the possibility of social reality as failure.*

I believe that bourgeois social reality is in a profound state of failure. The system depends on the reduction of persons to automatons, etc. Dehumanization is implicit in the property-dominated system, etc. That much is obvious and by now trite; what is less obvious is what happens to people who find new ways of dealing with the failed social reality. To explore this issue we have completely to re-evaluate Freud's ideas of 'higher' and 'lower' stages of development and have another look at the notions of fixation and frustration. If, for example,

* Admittedly some people find a purer conception of 'regression' in Freud's earlier writings, e.g. *The Interpretation of Dreams*, and believe that this was only distorted later because of his rigid rules of *practice*.

the higher is regarded as a more normal state in our society, the lower state may be one of heightened awareness. Also 'fixation' and 'frustration' may be intentional acts of refusal to move further along the path of normality – which is in fact a cul de sac.

Instead of speaking of regression, which is now nothing more than a pseudo-explanatory word, let us talk of *going back* or, sometimes, 'staying where you are' which, in a manically moving situation, can look like 'regression'. There are two modes of going back. One may go back *with the hope, or the prior internal promise, to return,** or one may go back with no hope or promise to return. In the latter case one is easily victimized by psychiatry – no hope means no defence against psychiatric violence. It is in the long-term interest of the psychiatric institution, which mirrors the interest of the outside society, to keep its inmates in a state of chronic infantilism – which may involve a coming and going of the inmates rather than permanent 'residence' in the hospital. It is by now a commonplace that bourgeois society needs a sub-population of lunatic-infants to define itself as normal and adult in contrast. If one goes back with the internal promise to return one still runs the risk that one's necessary project might be converted into psychiatric 'chronicity'. Once one is in the psychiatric system it is, to say the least, very difficult to extricate oneself from it. The stigma lasts – despite all the 'liberal' developments.

In terms of dealing with a 'going back' that is elected rather than imposed, the re-living in a new manner of a life gone wrong, 'even' the most 'advanced' therapeutic communities fail on some of these points that I shall

* One 'internal promise to return' is a condition of all good ecstatic experiences (a-noia) and also of symbiosis (mergence of two selves) in a relationship; there can be 'good' temporary symbioses.

catalogue – fail because they take into themselves all the historically intelligible but unnecessary fears of the world outside. I mean fear of social disturbance that might be blamed on the hospital in the form of lack of control, fear of sexuality and fear of suicide in both short- and long-term forms. Above all, fear of the person who simply tries to be alive with a true, crazy vitality that would by-pass the deadly, deadening trap of normality.

This catalogue of fearful psychiatric control includes some of these items: limitation for reasons of fear rather than care of free exit and entry, limitation of one's own control of one's money and few possessions, even sometimes one's watch, as in some prison systems. The limitation of communication with the outside world, e.g. having to get the resident doctor's permission to make or receive telephone calls or receive visitors. The total barring of sexuality, e.g. nurses persistently coming into the room or insisting on one's leaving the door open – many chronic 'neurotic' or 'psychotic' problems could be solved by a full and free sexuality (in any form) in privacy with free contraceptive guidance. Then there is the use of drugs as substitute life and substitute sexuality – not to mention more violent 'physical treatments' such as abreaction, electroshock or insulin which are still widely used. Finally the life-hating bureaucracy that takes the form of a medical and then lay chain of command which results, like the Nazi system, in no one finally taking responsibility for anything. Then finally the coercive community or group therapy sessions and occupational therapy, as if one had nothing better to do with one's time than submit oneself to this substitute family that replicates unknowingly all the forms of violence of one's family of origin by virtue of its coercive character.

In short, one dare not attempt to re-live one's life in

the prevalent system of fearful, desperate control – control that is ultimately a mass-societal fear reaction.

There is in fact the possibility of a true, face-to-face, human protection, but here the last word must be that of the person who goes back. Without this fundamental election of human protection on his part there is only a purely, passive, non-creative result. The trouble, whatever it is, repeats itself.

For a freely elected 'going back', with the internal promise to return, to work, there must be a deep decision underlying whatever extravagances going back necessitates. The human protection that I have referred to means the *availability* of other people, and not the coercive, compulsive, interfering presences of others. In non-institutional communes out in the community the same mistake of compulsive accompaniment is also too easily and too often made. The same fears that obtain in official therapeutic communities persist. A changing, i.e. non-institutionalized, charisma is needed. Unfortunately the charismatic person can only bear the situation for one or two years at the most. So a shifting charisma in any case comes about. The burden of mediating the interior of the commune and the 'outer world' is considerable, and the charismatic guide often goes back himself, in one sense or another, in the face of this strain. It may seem very simple, just being with another who is in a crisis of going back and listening to another's fantasies and dreams and witnessing his acts. Please take my word for it that it is the most difficult work on earth. Until the work becomes play.

When one considers going back it is ironic that one may have been more alive in the 'past' than in the 'present'. (I use inverted commas to emphasize the derived character of temporal concepts as well as spatial ones –

derivation from non-spatio-temporal *direction* in the sense that I have defined it.) Going back is the re-discovering of a lost past but it is more than simply rejuvenation. The acts involved in destructuring and then restructuring the present moment through a re-lived past permit a profound re-direction of the course of one's life. Part of this re-direction is the seeing through of the falsehood of social normality, and the relinquishing of aspirations to the fatal goal of 'good' adjustment. In principle one cannot generalize about the content of going back. One can only refer to actual individual instances.

One day in a hall above a bar where I was scheduled to produce 'happenings' of some sort or other, a girl arrived and haltingly told me that she wanted to speak to me about something very urgent. In the midst of the wild chaos I tried to hear her – or at least see her. She was quite tall and quite attractive with long blond hair and was probably about nineteen or twenty. Her blue jeans and sweater were grimy and falling to pieces around her, literally onto the floor. Neighbours had solicitously brought her along to that bar, knowing vaguely about some advertisement of the happenings that she seemed interested in. So she came, after an endless peregrination through various parts of Europe, from her home near Utrecht in Holland. Her name she said, and that was all she said, was Marja. She sat and waited while I spoke the things I minimally had to speak with other people – and those as usual were quite a lot. And then she just sat.

Later I pieced together the story. It was one of 'just sitting' – for several months in her room, neighbours occasionally bringing her food. She had been in psychiatric hospitals twice in Holland. On the first occasion she had had three or four electroshock treatments and drugs and close confinement. Her brother, who was a final-year medical student, told me that the diagnosis had been schizophrenia. On the second occasion she had been put into the hospital by the usual parent-doctor collusion and had just received tranquillizers until one day she walked out.

I was fascinated by her silence and her unchanging facial expression and immobility – and wasn't sure what to do about her. Finally I decided to take her home with me and see how things developed. So I did. She stayed with me about three weeks during which I fed her, made love with her, and then took her to work with me. At work she 'just sat' in the next room as I worked. And then she started to talk. And she never stopped talking except sometimes to sleep or to break my transistor radio because I was listening to the news. She would also wander out naked into other parts of the building. I mended a huge gaping hole in the seat of her jeans and began to feel very tired.

Finally I shared responsibilities with someone else in a close-by commune with which I was involved. Howard was a homosexual young man with extraordinary sensitivity, in whom I felt implicit trust. Marja shared a room nearby in a neighbourhood commune (i.e. several apartments whose occupants walked to meet each other at one central apartment) and carried on talking between three and five hours a day with Howard. The talk had the quality of her having just been born and then rapidly moving through the first three years. It was as if she had never talked before in her life. As regards content the issue was simple: she was thinking over all of her experience of those nearly twenty years and then thinking about the thinking so that somehow she might get the thinking and the thinking about the thinking together into one piece that would be Marja at last.

At the end of all this, after about four to five months,

she seemed to begin to accomplish this piecing together, and the critical evidence was that she was able to help other people and listen to them. The last I heard from her brother was that she was living independently, occasionally smoked hashish, about which she had learned in the commune, had a lover, had told him that she knew how never to get into the psychiatric game any more and when her parents got on to her she would just listen with care. And she would never mind them ever again. She would be untouchable by them and she would learn more and more how to touch.

I want to outline the conditions under which a true renewing experience of re-living one's life might occur. So often in 'post-Freudian' theory the same mistake has been made – the emphasis on normality as an ideal aim, from which one regresses backwards into some sort of past failure that one mistakenly regards as an achieved past life. This is a past that is better forgotten than remembered – a past that feeds off one's present life. I am speaking of a remembered past that consists solely in the not-learning of one's 'past life'. Or rather a false remembering of one's present life – false in so far as it aspires to social normality.

The conditions for a truly renewing going-back are in some respects like those for an LSD voyage. Firstly, the right human accompaniment is necessary. The accompanist must have had a profound 'regressive' experience herself or himself. *A total personal 'regressive' experience, risking social breakdown, is an essential part of the 'training' of any psychiatrist:* this is part of what I mean by anti-psychiatrist. Then, the accompanist must be capable of following – otherwise he does not know what he is speaking about – the Taoist principle of *wu-wei*, of non-interference while remaining as a very real presence; this amounts to a non-contradictory activity of positively 'doing nothing', of letting the other be in the plenitude of his experience. No rules are imposed on experience or action since no rules are necessary: in a situation of non-interference the person who goes back finds a personal discipline with no social norms but which is a self-regulation unique to the person in question, and which is the foundation of the discipline of the person newly made whole after the experience of going back. Only fear in the people accompanying the person going back generates a fear in him that can destroy this discipline. *We all need a witness* – someone who will see and listen to us without necessarily saying a word. But we know that they are knowing us, perhaps in some entirely unformulated way, and we know that they know that we know.

Then the right place is required. This should never be a psychiatric institution of any type, since even in the most enlightened clinics the medical model persists – the doctor–patient relationship, unbalanced in power terms, that excludes any mutuality in the sense of a free interchange of experience. Also psychiatrists very rarely have the personal experience of going back, and the experience of the reaction of others to such experience, that would give them freedom to move, without interfering, in the space of the person who is going back. Psychoanalysis is often regarded as a controlled, 'safe' way of going back but, however useful a good psychoanalytic experience might be (and there are some such experiences after all), it is totally different as an experience to actual going back. Different because of its rules, its nature as a process of control and its ultimate orientation to adjustment to the bourgeois system rather than profound change in one's way of being. The right setting for an experience of going back is a non-institutionalized commune located 'out' in the community.

Next, it is a question of the right time for going back. This time is difficult to detect but it is possible to form a judgement (oneself together with another person of sufficient experience) based on the clear feeling of having reached a saturation point with regard to a suffocating social normality. At the saturation point there may be a clear process of 'being driven mad by others' in operation, or one may make an autonomous *choice* (and I do not mean just sitting down and deciding) to go back because one has had enough of the perversion of one's existence by the exigencies of the normal world. As well as being sure of the right time to go back one has to be sure that one can take one's time in going back, whether it be a matter of days or months. Pressures to continue living one's usual life are very great and taking one's due time may seriously interfere with the basic practicalities both of one's own life and those of others who are close to one. This ultimately cannot be helped but the assistance of an experienced guide may be invaluable in paving one's way to an appropriate moment. But however personally opportune the moment might be it will always seem inopportune to most normal people who, if allowed near the scene, would try to bring about psychiatric punishment and imprisonment.

Another condition of going back is the imperative condition of prior extreme situations or 'near to death' experiences. By these experiences I do not mean literal experiences of being close to biological death (though this is one mode of entry into the possibility of going back). Extreme situations may arise with extreme relationship problems, with seemingly impossible choices in the family or other micro-social situations that madden one, or, as I have described in this book, with experiences with LSD or similar anti-drugs. Nearness to death in the sense of 'the last moment' is the point to regress from – not necessarily immediately but at one's right time. Otherwise what looks like going back may be pure self-infantilization which is the reverse of liberation: it is telling a lie in one's behaviour, acting the role of a child so as simply to be treated with indulgence; there is no prior agony of extreme experience.

Another prior condition to going back, ideally though not always possibly, is the cathartic act of 'talking out' one's family with an experienced other person over several meetings. This preliminary exorcism, if handled correctly, should not be a more or less interminable analytic process. It is a matter, perhaps, of realizing how *boring* one's family of origin is and how little there is to say about it (although the 'little' might be very important). The 'transference' and 'counter-transference' spoken of so much are usually (however abstractly justifiable) little more than conveniences that justify each actor getting into the insides of the other for an indefinite time. Transference and (in supervision) counter-transference interpretation is a cosy co-inhabitation that would, in the macro-social interest, finally deny the separateness and autonomy of persons. I am not denying the usefulness or even the temporary necessity of statements in the form of transference/counter-transference interpretation – as long as such statements are made in an open relationship context, free of needs to control and needs to be controlled, which is developed by an essentially non-verbal attunement of the existence of each to that of the other. I am, however, stressing the dangers of this form of interpretation – including the danger to the therapist who because of her or his fear cannot do without a defensive mode of getting, and remaining, under the skin of the other. The sacrifice of the reality of the 'patient' is too high a price to pay.

'Talking out' one's family is only too easily obstructed by transference interpretation.

Finally, an essential preparation for going back is learning fully to recount one's dreams to another. Dream content closely approximates the going back experience, also the 'art' of carrying a dream through to its end is closely related to the emergence of a new self at the end of the experience of going back. This proper concluding of dreams may have to be learned in the right sort of therapy.

Without the right dream one cannot properly go back and return.

To retain important dreams one has to achieve an attitude to one's dreams by which one gives them their proper value and centrality. To capture a rapidly disappearing dream on awakening one might for a while, until one no longer needs this resource, have to wake up whoever one is sleeping with to register the dream in the mind of the other. The Sènoi tribe in Borneo live communally and achieve a wise, pacific and problem-free tribal life by a simple procedure: every morning they have a session in which they recount their dreams to each other to achieve a therapeutic sharing of experience and also learn how to carry certain dreams further. For example, if one has a dream of falling and then either switches off the dream content or wakes up, one has to learn to fall further and further in subsequent dreams until one achieves a revelatory feeling about the significance of The Fall for oneself, and also what it is one is falling into or out of. Also, if one has dreams of imminent death, my experience has been that 'dream prescriptions'* to dream

* By 'dream prescription' I mean sustained meditation on whatever dream elements seem particularly important, with a view to developing them in subsequent dreams. One is accompanied in this meditation by another person, who may have dreamed further than

out fully the death and decay of one's body, and then its regeneration, are necessary.

In summary we might say that we go back when we stop what stops us going back.

As well as, and related to, re-living one's life there is the phenomenon of *pre-living* one's life. *There are, I believe, 'present' modes of experiencing the 'future'* that challenge usual notions of the progression of time. A phenomenological re-examination of Freud's screen-memories may help introduce this subject. In dealing with the problem of childhood amnesia Freud reached the conclusion that, just as the adult, the child retains in memory only that which is important. Through 'condensation' and 'displacement' these fragments of childhood recollection are represented in adult memory by apparently trivial things. A thorough analysis can bring out from these childhood recollections (screen-memories) much of what has been forgotten.

Things can often work like this, however: a man in his early forties had had four principal 'living with' relationships with women (apart from transient 'affairs'), each for a period of two years or more, and was now commencing his fifth. He came to see me because he feared that there might be some sort of repetitive pattern in his relationships that had led to their termination and that unknowingly he might repeat the pattern in his present relationship. After several meetings he remembered a situation that had existed before he was five years old and which he had forgotten during all the subsequent years. He had had five soft animal dolls that he insisted on taking to

oneself, with whatever words that may seem necessary being exchanged between the two. Freud had a dream in which he dissected his pelvis; as a further dream to explore the nature of sexuality, I can recommend one of dissecting one's own head – and then kicking it away.

bed with him arranged in a series on his pillow. Gradually, as the dolls became ragged and dirty, his mother threw them away one by one until he was left with only one, a smiling monkey doll called Bimbo. He would never accept losing Bimbo. But of course one day his mother took away the beloved monkey and he spent a day in tears. He told me how he liked to call the very attractive woman he presently lived with 'Monita' (Spanish for 'little monkey') and he began to realize how he connected her warm smile and her softness with the favourite fifth doll his mother had taken away. He feared that by some mysterious means his mother or something that represented her would deprive him of his beloved Monita (in fact in his previous four 'marital' experiences his drinking cognac had played a central role in ending the relationships, the cognac representing, amongst other things, the bad feeding aspect of his mother). With the fifth woman he was finally free to throw away the relationship himself or not. I do not want to dwell on the obvious psychoanalytic significances of all this but simply to focus on the directional sense of what went on. One might say that the future of the man with 'his' women was present in the experience of the child with his dolls. The implication seems to me to be that if one could progressively sort through the distortions of present experience one could increasingly experience one's future as present. Ultimately one might *experience* one's 'future' death as a present event. Thus we may remove false terror and mistake from the future.

In short: regression despite its scientific aura is a dirty word. To go back and re-live our lives is natural and necessary. A society that denies what is natural and necessary must be terminated by whatever means are natural and necessary.

IO

On Knowing Where You Stand

Mental hospitals flourish on uncertainty – what treatment one is going to receive, what ward one is going to be transferred to, whether or not one is going to be discharged – or if one is ever going to be discharged. It is something like certain Jewish prisoners in the last war who were told, to induce submission, that they were going to be castrated at the other end of the journey (in fact what they got was death). The same thing happens to political prisoners in South America by constant transfer from one gaol to the next. In prison they take away one's watch and put one in a dark cell so that one knows neither the time of day nor which day it is – also one does not know which prisoner is going to be taken out of the cell next for interrogation or torture.

In the case of two-person uncertainty: in woman-man relations the man often does not take the 'trouble' to define the erotogenic zones of the woman and therefore simply uses her sexually. There is no mutuality of experience in this penis-centred pseudo-sexuality.

Another form of two-person uncertainty arises from the importation into the relationship of unresolved problems derived from the 'family of origin'. This is different from the problems produced by 'internalized' family figures that I shall discuss later in this chapter. In this case the actual mother, father and siblings are present usually the mother being more subtly active in undermining the woman-man relationship – because of her envy, jealousy, distrust of men and her feeling either that women should stick together in the case of a mother-daughter relationship, or, in the case of a mother-son relationship, that her son is an indispensable part of her body-mind.

The whole point about the simple uncertainty principle in human relations is that of *relativity to the other*. If one defines oneself in terms of the attributions of others one will never know where one stands. It is only by discovering the true single and singular ground of one's being in aloneness that one might find out where one stands. All relative being is being that must inevitably be destroyed by uncertainty. *Self*-centred being progressively withstands all attempts to undermine it by uncertainty, but becoming self-centred (the opposite of egocentric) is a long and arduous battle. Many people think that they act from the centre of themselves when it is clear that they do not. The slightest breeze of uncertainty will blow them off their ontological feet.

I have so far stressed uncertainty between persons. There is of course also uncertainty that arises within a person due to the action of 'internalized' past or present people or bits of people or due to an autonomous otherness that has nothing to do with actual others. Autonomous otherness is proven by exhaustive analysis of individual persons where one finds an irreducible care – a core of being that cannot be reduced to the more or less easily intelligible machinations of internalized others. The autonomous otherness that generates this sort of uncertainty can only be understood as an internalization of the mystifications and the mysteries by the whole society, world, cosmos. In these terms there is evidently quite enough to be uncertain about. The 'persecutory superego' may not be intelligible in terms of experience of parental or ancestral persons, but may only be intelligible in terms of a profound internalization of the oppressive and repressive aspects of the whole society.

Also, certain people generate uncertainty in themselves (and, or not, in others) because they *need* it to avoid some greater feared catastrophe. They just do not want to know where they stand because they fear that the ground they find themselves standing on might be too precarious a promontory. One problem is that they may be right and the therapeutic risk is to help the person look down at where his feet are – and hope for the best. Many fears brought to therapy are only too justified objectively and cannot be reduced to the operations of 'unconscious phantasy'. Therapists work in bad faith if they try to 'interpret away' such fears – interpretation is then simply a defence against the therapists' own fears that have become confused with those of the other. The fears of 'not being able to help' and 'not being able to be helped' can be mutually destructive. But we have to face it: many people have the original project of not being able to be helped, and many therapists lack the capacity to help in a socially effective way, i.e. a way in which micro-politics and macro-politics form a *continuum* with no ideological interruptions of this *continuum*.

Most basically, uncertainty arises when limits are placed on our actions by others – with the best intentions in the world. This loss of autonomy may prove fatal unless one can switch it into self-election, defining one's own limits and the territory on which one stands. No compromise is possible. All the well-intentioned acts of others vitiate essential autonomy. Ultimately everyone else matters but no one else counts – the score of one's life.

I have written in this and previous chapters about the modes of mystification induced by mental hospitals. I would like to deal now with the uncertainties generated by 'therapeutic communities'. The mystification here is immense. There seems to be free entry and exit but in fact there is a subtle control of these movements. Sexes mix freely but there is a (usually) unspoken taboo against sexual relations in direct body terms. This springs from the staff's fear of their own sexuality, from the staff's need to infantilize the 'patients' by regarding them as irresponsible children for whom they are *in loco parentis* and by the conscious need to stop the propagation of 'psychosis', 'neurosis' and 'psychopathy' in terms of some vague eugenic attitude. In each case there is a perpetuation of the false sickness/health dichotomy and the perpetuation of the condition that is supposed to be 'treated'. This more or less subtle perpetuation of an original damage serves the society in which the therapeutic community functions very well despite occasional conflicts with outside authority. The equation is simple: social madness perpetuated = normality perpetuated. So the patients get anti-sex drugs, phenothiazines and barbiturates etc., and any sort of 'good normal' (not 'normal normal') life is lost forever. Forever because patients, like pet dogs, are trained to be faithful to their medical masters. There are sexually mixed wards but this is merely a sort of male and female prick-teasing because the prohibitions against sexual relations remain as strong as ever – between patients and patients, patients and staff and patients and visitors. Time and time again I have heard indoctrinated patients defend this vicious system. They don't know any longer for one instant where they stand.

Another area of basic uncertainty is suicide. This is an area hedged with binds of all sorts. There seems to be no purity in suicide as an act which is why so many kill themselves 'by accident'. There are a host of possible interpretations as to why one might kill oneself. No freedom is left for the act. Also it seems virtually impossible to kill oneself without aggression against someone. There can be no suicide free of guilt or 'self-indulgence' and while many people will tell you why not to do it no one will advise you, without a trace of aggression, on the best way for you to do it. At the last moment of your life you stand alone and you don't know where you stand. The right to kill oneself should be absolute and there should be suicide accompanists to help clarify (not negatively interpret) *why* one is killing oneself but not stop one. I happen to think that, even in situations of torture and terminal cancer, *suicide is always a mistake*, but the right to kill oneself must remain absolute. The mistake lies in the deprivation of even painful experience and in the fact that one is acting without knowing where one stands.

In short, the induction of uncertainty, not knowing where one stands, is easily come by. It is precisely in these moments, when one is most 'down', oppressed and depressed, that one has to find the courage to struggle on from the obscure moment to a clear moment.

When one knows where one stands one is in a position to realize *the importance of acting without thinking*. This means acting without deliberation (which leads one away from liberation) but acting from a base of *preliberation*. The liberation of preliberation issues from the gratuitous choice (gratuitous in the sense of the negation of all restrictive conditioning) to know that where one stands is Where One Is.

11

On Ending Relationships

In writing here of relationships I include the psycho-analytic relationship in so far as this achieves the status of a relationship – for example one of the most eminent politically *avante garde* psychoanalysts in the world sits at a desk twelve feet away from 'his' patient' (who lies on the couch) facing the other way and, despite the lack of any face-to-face encounter, sincerely believes that he is work-ing on a relationship, transference or whatever, while in fact there is no beginning of relationship and so there can be no end – interminable analysis. Hence there issue many papers on the 'criteria for termination of analysis'.

In considering the ending of relationships we have to recognize a certain truth: the state of being 'fed-up' with the relationship refers to a total mutuality of 'appetite', but this equality is usually hidden in one of the partners and may only be disclosed by a certain amount of thera-peutic work, though not as much as therapists generally make out, if the approach is correct, i.e. totally free of the non-therapeutic mystifications that are so common in officially designated therapy (as distinct from the 'spon-taneous' therapy of our day-to-day relationships). The state of being fed-up is the state of being satiated with work one has done on one's self in the relationship and therefore on the relationship. It also means that one has eaten up the other enough. The alimentary metaphor is appropriate since it brings out the idea of the oral appropriation of each by the other and hence reveals the property and consumption base of all relationships in a bourgeois society. A few of us may alter our styles of life sufficiently to partially escape from this situation but for most a revolutionary change in the whole society will be necessary to relate to each other with a full humanity.

The work done in a relationship can be made clear to the point where we can decide whether the work has been carried to its *natural limit*. There is a natural limit to relationship work and this natural limit is defined (as Sartre so well describes it in *Saint Genet*) as an original choice of being. Beyond that moment of illumination of the natural limit each of us is free to let the other be. After this sort of ending of relationship work both are free to love each other the rest of their lives whether they live together or not. *No relationship significantly entered can ever end* – the trouble is with the significant entry.

But I should give some example of an original choice that defines the natural limit of a specific relationship. It's a common enough example. Laura, aged 29, had an intensely strong, though socially concealed, relationship with her mother – it seemed that her mother was no longer particularly important in her life. Her father was alive as a weak 'absent' presence – as is the wont of bourgeois fathers. In her twenties she had three significant, as apart from casual, relationships with men, each of which lasted for about two years. Each relationship ended explosively. In the fourth relationship things became clearer to the 'observer' ('me'). Her original choice of mother (with whom she had now achieved a relationship of more than parity since she had to some extent mothered her mother in moments of the latter's weakness) entailed preferential relations with women, with increasing frustration of the fourth man who was blind enough about his own mother to enter a full collusion with her. She wanted to live in a feministic universe rather than a male-orientated one. This involved spending much time with other women – 'just talking', although the just talking, metaphorically, was mutual masturbation. With the man her orgasms were centred on digital clitoral stimulation, not penile penetration – to her and his increasing frustration. She chose to see a female analyst (he was already seeing an analyst without illumination) with whom she formed a close symbiosis in which the analyst confirmed that all her actions and experiences were 'right'. She also maintained her relationship with her mother at a safe but warm distance. The relationship reached its end – its natural limit – when the man, after a violent scene involving the mother, entered hospital with a severe, 'immovable' depression. The original choice of a woman had determined the natural limit of the relationship with the fourth man (as it had in different ways with the previous three). The just end, however painful, had been reached. Both subsequently gained illumination about all that had happened and established a good non-collusive relationship though not living together.

This 'case' had to do with a failure of wholeness or holiness in what have now become the usual glib terms of putting it. It is a case of a marriage 'ending badly', but the maintenance of the original choice, unshiftable in a particular psychoanalysis, necessitated, via the natural limit, the end. *Holy matrimony should perhaps be more holy (whole) and less matrimonial.* That is why I would propose a sacramental marriage rather than marriage that is legally contractual with or without the connivance of an established church. By sacramental marriage I mean marriage based on a profound experience of relationship in which a vow is implicitly or explicity taken – and this vow is recognized – a vow to work through the relationship to its natural limit. In legally imposed marriage the law comes between the partners and fractures the relationship from the start. In this case the *first* letter from a lawyer signals the end of a relationship if not the end of the institution of marriage. It is a moral imperative now that *all pressures into legal marriage have to be resolutely resisted – external or internal pressures.*

I have written earlier of significant entry into relationship. Such significant entry may be achieved in certain psychoanalyses but is by no means the rule. The limits imposed by the analytic initiation usually make the attainment of a natural limit of relationship impossible – hence all the controversy that I have referred to about the criteria for termination of analysis. For one thing, as far as medical analysts are concerned, some overturning of the rules of medical 'ethics' is necessary – these make therapy as 'a making whole' a *lie**. How can sexual relations between analyst and analysand or therapist and therapeutized be excluded *in principle* from any whole relationship? If fact it is simply a matter of appropriateness to the situation and – if sexuality happens – the timing is crucial. Bed therapy may be the only right move at a certain critical junction according to a coincidence of needs of both people concerned. Sexuality is essentially

---

* I am not advocating that these rules be broken (this could be just another abuse of the power of the medical role) but that the ethical situation be revised. In a recent questionnaire thirteen per cent of doctors on the West Coast of the USA felt that sexual relations with patients might sometimes be positive. As the incidence of impotence in the remaining eighty-seven per cent was unknown, this figure might be significant.

an exploration of archaic zones of bodily experience involving, beyond the tactile and kinesic areas, vision, smell, taste and sound. Many people are held paralysed in more than one of these sensory modalities and release can only come in terms of direct experience and not 'talking cure'. Interminable analysis is the direct and obvious result imposed by the original rules of the analytic context. Against all the odds, to reach the end-point of a relationship one has to carry on working beyond the moment of inviting rest – beyond the point where we feel too tired to continue. To relax in this way is to invite incompletion of the relationship.

The end entails an optimism. Remember that someone once said 'the beginning is in the end'. Remember once again that no relationship significantly entered into is ever completed throughout one's life. There may be an end to living together but the feeling goes on or even increases. Marriages may be dissolved, but the dissolution of relationships is illusion.

When we come to the beginning and end of political relationships on the macro-level of personal involvement we are dealing with a different order of events. Here relationships are felt to be dependent on each person *not seeing* the other. It's a dangerous presupposition that revolutionary movements can occur *and continue* as revolution without due regard to what goes on concretely between actual persons who face each other (the micro-political). Why, for instance, as I have mentioned before, did Lenin not adequately (though he belatedly glimpsed it) see how, under his nose, Stalin was extending his control over the incipient bureaucracy while Trotsky was trying to perpetuate and extend the revolution? Without a full and proper insight into the beginning of a human process the vision fails to penetrate through to its end. It was very different in China where Mao Tse-tung and a small group of comrades who really got to know each other in Hunan started to collect the people around them. One has just to compare the Russian and the Chinese revolutions. And then again the Cuban revolution: Fidel and his small band in Mexico got to know each other intimately before finally setting out on the Granma. These relationships were carried through to the end – the end of death – of Camilo Cienfuegos and Che and many of the other comrades. The ideal of continuous revolution depends on relationships being properly commenced and carried through to their natural limits – only too often death, in the case of revolutionaries.

Relationships between political activists may also be ended by a failure of nerve. The fibres of the political nerve tear apart. Only concrete work on *relationships* between people can obviate this.

There is a very practical issue involved here if one particularly looks at young student activists. There is a polarization of activism and personal insight. In reality there is no necessary conflict. It is easy for the personally insightful to regard the 'pure' activist as emotionally blind. It is equally easy for activists to regard those who seek for an understanding of subtle personal issues as being both cowardly and introspective – and introspection as we know is a 'bourgeois habit'. In fact this polarization is simply a conventional device of our bourgeois, imperializing, ruling élite. If they divide us they rule us.

If they have done it to Africa and Asia and South America they can divide-and-rule us further. They can, further, divide and rule workers and students as happened during the 1968 rebellion in France – which is why a beautiful rebellion failed to be a revolution. So we see that the central revolutionary activism must be acts of union.

On every level of both small group and mass action the end is in the beginning.

Let's begin to make the end right.

And then we might begin.

12

The Re-Invention of Love

Firstly, I would like to differentiate between love and compassion. Love is essentially a two-person situation, though any person may be involved in several such two-person situations, whereas compassion may extend to most people in the world and even embrace the cosmos. Love entails a total involvement with and total commitment to the other along with the most central, though not necessarily exclusive, sexual involvement. This is more or less the standard version of love but one which has to be destructured and then restructured. I shall examine the process of destructuring and restructuring, along with other issues, in this chapter. The standard version of love can no longer hold because of its limitations.

The 'feeling with' of compassion is another story. Compassion is not merely love multiplied, it is not merely love mixed with pity, it is not merely a more distanced love. Compassion is a radical modification of the spirit that entails the disappearance of merely personal violence and it potentiates rather than reduces one's revolutionary possibilities. It is certainly universalizing in so far as one may feel like weeping at the sight of old, 'ugly', poor or crippled people in the street – though one weeps only internally as a rule. Compassion, too, is a deep sorrow for the pain of another – sorrow when the more usual response, regrettably, is to feel oneself secretly elevated by witnessing suffering – that is feeling sorry rather than sorrow. (Being sorry for someone is always destructive, identificatory self-indulgence whereas sorrow implies separateness of being.) Compassion in this sense is preconditioned by the presence of love for actual other specific people. But as I said in the introduction to this book there can be no compassion for the enemies of compassion.

Historically, and very schematically, we may examine the love of the esoteric, 'left-handed' *tantra*. Or rather we may not examine it because it is esoteric, but I can say that the sexual *yoga* involves, temporarily, the total loss of one's 'normal' mind – the state that I have referred to as anoia.* Love here involves a repeated movement between being in our minds (enoia) and being beyond our minds (anoia).

The Platonic notion of love, as the force by which the soul, awakened to perfect Beauty, approaches immortality, was lost in the historical reality of Greek society by a reduction to pure body.

Christian love placed love of Christ, that remote other, before love of another, present person. Making love was venial, sinful unless blessed by a representative of Christ on earth. This 'blessing' inevitably became involved with the state, the law, property and money. The whole system became a diffuse punishment and an evil antithesis to the love that we must talk about and live now.

In courtly love, despite moments of defiance, there was finally a submission to a hierarchy of power and the reduction of love to ritualized gesture.

In Victorian love the money emphasis reached its peak. Possession meant that the wife became entirely the pro-

* See *The Death of the Family*, Chapter 1.

perty of the husband. Only in the year of 1972 in Austria, that sophisticated European power, has the position slightly changed. Until now, if the husband moved from place to place a wife had to follow him at the risk of being eliminated as a person in society.

In the case of love in bourgeois society today there is a mystification. Ultimately there is an emphasis on legal marriage and the money aspect persists in a more ritualized but very real form. The fact of unmarried people living together and having children is more or less overlooked in most bourgeois societies but often has to be disguised in various ways, so that one can never be quite secure about one's position. In any case the rule of the day is to form the bourgeois nuclear family, that monstrous tool of the repressive state which, in its very nature, presents situations of fear that deny love. Another mystification is revealed when we look at the dominant micro-political ideology of our time that lays claim to explaining human experience: Freudian theory has nothing to say about love. Libido rules a territory where love fears to tread.

Then of course there is revolutionary love – love of comrades fighting for the people and love of the people – not an abstract 'people' but people one meets and works with. When Che Guevara talked of love being at the centre of revolutionary endeavour he meant both. For people like Che or George Jackson love was the prime mover of their struggle and love cost them both their lives. Love coupled with immense pride. Malcolm X, Carlos Marighela – the list runs on.

Short of direct revolutionary activism, communes provide the key to a new form of love. Sexual sharing, though only when it is not an escape from the *work* of a central two-person relationship, and also occasionally multiple love-making, between people who know and love each other without the impersonality of the orgy, show the way to a non-jealous, non-possessive non-property-orientated love – *though sexual sharing is by no means essential to the commune*. It demonstrates what I have called *The Illusion of the Quantifiability of Love*. If person A loves (and makes love with) person B (who may be A's constant partner) and if A loves (and makes love with) person C, then A's love for C subtracts nothing from A's love for B. Subtraction, loss, is the illusion. How things work in an ideal commune accords with this realization. Things get fouled up, however, if A's relationship with C has an aggressive intent against B who in turn responds with some sort of aggression against A and C.

I have found often, for instance, that if a young man with a so-called 'primal scene' problem gets into the bed in which there is an older man with a woman with whom he has just made love and makes love with the same woman (though only if and when this is acceptable to all concerned), there is a great release of tension regarding 'parent figures' as well as an acceptable release of homosexual tensions – the 'phantasy' in the young man being the equation 'I fuck his woman = I am fucked by him'. Only mutual fear can produce bad crises.

In fact all this has nothing much to do with mere fucking (i.e. the most limited aspect of the whole body component) but is a matter of everyone *loving* and *proving the acceptability of the 'unacceptable'*. In terms of love and sexuality it can thus be shown in body terms, beyond verbal terms, that there is far less to fear than is generally believed. The 'talking cure' cannot effect this deteriorization of love and sexuality.

Another commune example was a couple with 'severe

sexual difficulties', the central element of which was the girl's fear of being raped by her father and 'of course' her wish to be raped. Everyone in the commune was making love at the time. While the young man of the couple was with another woman in the same room an older man gently made love with his wife and then they all slept peacefully together. The next morning the couple were grateful and all embraced. They had to leave shortly for another country (most of the communes I have worked in have had a shifting international population – which helps disseminate the commune idea) and proceeded to have a baby – with love.

The greatest fear of all has nothing to do with hatred and aggressive acts. *The greatest fear is of loving and being loved*. In the curious contortions of the mind love becomes equated with madness. Love is felt to be total loss of self which becomes equated with a dreaded madness. This is true of the act of loving even at times when orgasm is not involved in the experience. If we can learn by some sort of therapeutic experience, by no means necessarily a professional experience (in fact it is less common in professional therapy), to accept this loss of self with surety beforehand about the return of self, we are open to love. Love has been lost and has to be re-invented. Love is a structure that has been falsely destructured through the development of property as mediation of human relations. It is only through a destructuring of the resultant false structure, by a change in property-relations, that love can be re-invented. This change can only occur through commune development or quantitative steps towards the qualitative revolutionizing of the whole society. Of course commune development is only one of the paths leading towards this qualitative change. We the people will be forced by repression into other counter-violent strategies and tactics. It would be ridiculous in most third-world countries to speak of communes as a principal means of struggle. There are exceptions to this, e.g. Argentina, but in general the violence of the oppressive system forces the people into urgent and desperate immediate counter-violence. There is no significant pre-revolutionary phase between total oppression and total revolution. Of course communes of sorts already exist in third-world countries but they cannot be oriented to any great extent to the elucidation of 'inner lives'.

If we are to strike the keynote of the New Love, I believe we shall find it in the act of *letting the other be*. This requires a restraint that may be very painful in the learning of it and, as we know, many relationships break up because one cannot let the other be. Letting be is not a psychological concept but an ontological one. It involves a change in our being, not changing our minds. *Not only is freedom the recognition of necessity but we have to recognize the necessity of recognizing freedom*. It is not paradoxical that one may have a total commitment to one central relationship and simultaneously have other loving (and possibly sexual) relations with others.

A spiritual seduction without bodily sexuality can be a centrally mystifying experience. The former, in my experience, can be more devastating, precisely because it is less obvious, than the latter, and the results more explosive. It certainly does not let the other be. Spiritual seduction is not necessarily an intentional act, but rather a degree of it is almost an inevitability in any commune group. Whoever happens to be the charismatic leader of the group at any time will inevitably attract members of the opposite and the same sex. The danger is that the leader colludes, knowingly or unknowingly, with this attraction. If this happens, the group becomes sterile and unproductive, except maybe for one or two lucky accidents. This is the case both with externally orientated (macro-political) communes and with more internally orientated communes (the commune ideal being of course a synthesis of both orientations).

In short, love can only be re-invented through the abolition of the bourgeois nuclear family that has destroyed it. The family must be replaced by communes in which sex is not regarded as private property. What passes for love in bourgeois family life is nothing less than political reaction. The Spanish word for son-in-law is *hijo político*. Legalized family relations are political and they are reactionary politics. The philosophical assumption, 'human nature cannot change', becomes an implicit family rule against change. One young man I knew in England went to a psychiatrist because he felt persecuted by his mother-in-law beyond all bounds of his possible acceptance. On the psychiatrist's advice (implicit after full case investigation) he emigrated to Australia. In Australia he embarked upon free-fall parachuting as an ultimate challenge to his desperation (disguised as his death). One day as he was free-falling he caught a glimpse of his mother-in-law falling past him. She opened her parachute last, he was only just lucky enough to remember to open his.

To love love one's self enough to love another involves one in passing beyond the pathos of the bourgeois family and the pathos of the first attempts at commune formation that we experience now, to the love that lies in truth on the other side of the revolution that we must make.

Against all the odds I choose to remain optimistic. For love to be re-invented what is required is not a change in socially visible attitudes but a change in being that then becomes socially apparent; I have experienced such changes in people although they are rare enough – manifesting as the transition from a possessive mode of being to a justly proud, non-predatory way of living out relations in full autonomy.

So, For Love and Revolution.

13

The Transpositions of Meditation

Those who devote themselves both to life in the world
and to meditation, by life in the world
overcome death, and by meditation achieve immortality.
Isha Upanishad

Meditation is often regarded by the politically active as
having to do with some sort of oriental quietism and therefore having nothing to do with, or even being flatly
opposed to, revolutionary work. This is far from the
truth as I hope to show, or at least indicate, here from
experiences in group meditation that I have had in various
cities, including Buenos Aires. This last city seemed important to me since here one finds concentrated many
common factors of problematic between first- and third-
world cultures. It is only unfortunate that the experiences
were limited to middle-class intellectuals, including briefly
one group of people professionally engaged in therapy,
but at the same time I believe that the politically active
people in this sector of society can perhaps benefit most
of all from meditation at this particular time.

It is neither desirable nor possible to attempt to trans-
plant Eastern forms of meditation to cultures with totally
different socio-economic forms of life, but I felt that, during an experimental introductory phase, it might be pos-

sible to trans*pose* an original spiritual tone into a new spiritual key.

The aim was for people to achieve a detachment from illusory problems, particularly from the enslaving time = money equation, so as to be able to confront more freely real problems which demand action. The meditation experience destructures both clock-time and the subjective sense of time. On the basis of this temporal change people might discover zones of time for *action* other than *activity* that earns money. This is particularly important with groups of people who can free time for political work by vastly reducing their exaggerated consumer needs. Personal change beyond intellectual political analysis is needed and meditation can play a part in a radical transformation of the whole bourgeois style of life.

The sessions varied in frequency from once to three times a week for a particular group at fixed times. I would give a brief introduction explaining the aim of acquiring the capacity to turn off one's mind and, through achieving this 'no-mind' state, approaching the possibility of merging with Voidness. This leads one to the increasing possibility of detachment from the systematized series of illusions that we have been conditioned to regard as 'reality'. Liberation from illusoriness leaves one freer to act in the world and extend liberation to every sphere of that which is human and indeed to all nature which we subject to ecological destruction. I would then refer to the fear that some people might feel in the unusual situation and say that of course anyone was free to leave quietly but would ask people not to come in late.

The physical situation was a quiet, dark room large enough for up to twenty people to sit, without there being any question of distracting bodily contact with each other. Incense was burnt to produce a uniform, neutral smell. I would ring a bell to mark the commencement of meditation and again after an hour to mark the end; this relinquishing of time-control was in itself important, though difficult for people used to controlling the time of others. The floor was carpeted but there were no chairs; people would sit cross-legged on the floor, those with previous experience possibly adopting a half-lotus position. The posture itself would produce discomfort in the legs and back after a time in many people; although one could change position I suggested that people experience the discomfort and then try to get inside the pain since if one got inside the pain, without refusing it, the pain could not be inside oneself.

Meditation of course was in total silence and to aid the process of emptying one's mind I burnt a candle at one end of the room, next to me, and suggested that people might concentrate on the flame of the external candle. After a while they might switch their concentration to an internal candle and then, as a final step, 'extinguish' the internal candle.

After the hour, for a fifteen-minute period people who had had experiences that cut across their meditation would talk about those experiences. Some people, for instance, would have tried compulsively to work out some problem in their lives and if the 'entry' of the problem was too great, I would suggest that they did not refuse the problem but concentrated on it (as in the case of a pain) without trying to understand it or work it out; thus they might enter the problem so that it would not be intruding into them. The work of 'solving problems' belongs to another situation, not meditation.

Then again, other people had curious changes of body image, for example experiencing some parts of their body as huge and other parts as absurdly small or non-existent.

Some would experience themselves as floating an infinite distance away, while others had more frightening experiences, for example a woman who felt her vagina changing into a hideous purple and brown object until, after she had managed to stay with the experience and accept her fear and revulsion, her body returned to its normal state. The parallels with 'psychedelic' experiences are obvious.

The result of a number of sessions was that most people experienced a greater fluency of movement in and out of their minds and also overcame the normal mechanistic opposition between 'inner' and 'outer' that is imposed on experience by intellection. Also, in some, there was a shift downwards from the cerebral to lower energy centres expressed as greater genital aliveness.

After a number of sessions people would have less to talk about after meditation and the exchanges would be largely non-verbal. Someone, for instance, might make a gesture towards me (or anyone else) or adopt a certain stance; one would then respond spontaneously with a gesture or stance that seemed to meet that of the protagonist. Or, again, it might be a subtle eye-exchange or exchange of sounds that would be hardly noticeable in ordinary social situations but which in this situation are highly sensitive forms of meeting and recognition which one can carry out into new social situations.

There is no question of understanding and interpreting 'group dynamics' or 'transference' in the post-meditation meeting (this was difficult for the professional therapists to grasp at first). Spontaneous *responses* open up new areas of social experience and new forms of meeting.

A considerable danger, however, is the problem of subsequent loss of what has been gained in and immediately after meditation sessions. The return to alienated situations of work and relationships is an inevitable threat. I found this after twice-daily meditation over periods of about two weeks at a stretch (with many months in between) at the Tibetan Buddhist monastery in Scotland. However, working with a continuous system of between one and three meditation sessions a week, going on for many months, the risk of loss is lessened – even in a hectic urban centre. Regularity is all-important and one person in a particular group should be able to make the requisite large room available regularly to the group (needless to say no one pays to meditate!). Gradually in between sessions people use their group experience to start meditating alone. One may then acquire the possibility of producing very brief no-mind states at any time – walking along the pavement, in a restaurant and so on. One is detached from one's body momentarily and experiences a deep trust before the anoia that one's body will automatically function and respond with full efficiency.

Approaching total voidness does not mean ultimate mergence with the Void. There must be a promise to return to the world, less afraid of death, of orgasm and of madness. One is then freer to act on every level of one's own being and of social being to change the world.

Moving out of our minds, which are really *their* minds, is the truest first step that leads us into and through liberated struggle.

14

Experience to the Guillotine

There are many techniques by which we may murder our experience. The society we live in obligingly provides the canvas on which we paint our acts of murder, and also the brush and paints – but *we* execute the painting. I intend to explore one mode of this execution by a series of apparently disconnected, but I hope not incoherent, statements in this chapter and the next.

Addiction, a 'major problem' of bourgeois* time(s), comes from the Latin *addictus* – assigned by decree, made over (past participle passive of *addicere* from *ad+dicere* – appoint, allot). There is an etymological sense of trying to speak *to* someone *through* something. It is the effort to discover a mediated communication when direct communication seems finally impossible, but it is an effort with

* By bourgeois I mean (and it's about time to specify at least roughly my usage of this term) essentially the classical marxist conception. The bourgeoisie in a fully developed capitalist society is the ruling class that rules or rather misrules and exploits through its ownership of the means of production. Dialectically interrelated with such socio-political definitions, however, is a certain life style, characterized by a global non-seeing of what is unreified human being, that we may describe as bourgeois. There are of course the workers in the first-world countries in particular, who have been swallowed up in the process of bourgeoisification that aims to obliterate the sense of class but generates false needs.

a built-in division between the impulses to failure (death) and success (new life). It is also an effort that is assigned to us, enforced on us by an external social reality that needs a certain number of us to be in this position.

There are more and less evident forms of addiction. The more evident forms are the so-called 'hard drugs', e.g. heroin, alcohol, barbiturates, amphetamines and to a lesser extent nicotine. The defining characteristic of hard drugs, despite a number of other characteristics, is the phenomenon of the agony of withdrawal from the drug, a phenomenon that does not obtain with cannabis, LSD, mescaline, DMT (dimethyltryptamine), psilocybin, and other 'psychedelic' substances.

Less evident forms of addiction include, firstly, compulsive seeking out of relationships that are contradictory to one's obvious needs; the difficulties in grasping what is obvious, however, are notoriously immense. One of the main tasks of good therapy is the achievement of clarity about the repeated election of 'wrong' relationships. The withdrawal experience from this state of affairs may be less clearly defined but just as devastating as withdrawal from hard drugs, and the resolution of the problem may be equally long term.

Secondly, there is addiction to psychoanalysis – an interminable symbiosis when each person gets under the skin of the other and feeds off the 'nutriment' of each other's body and mind. Conventional interpretations and dream analysis may simply intensify the symbiosis and mutual dependence rather than lead the way to separateness. Becoming separate persons is an issue of concrete actions on both 'sides' and not merely verbal responses to experience – however 'intelligent' the responses. This problem of symbiosis ensues most often from a political (as I define or rather describe it in the first chapter) disjunction between the two persons – or group analyst and group. From my personal experience in my own first analysis this is painfully clear to me. The analyst lived a wealthy, highly controlled and eminently respectable bourgeois family life while I, having given up a lucrative, though to some extent illuminating and emotionally rewarding, practice in Harley Street, London, would be sleeping on the floor in shared rooms in various communes in that city. The analyst very evidently could not stomach my way of life and could barely conceal his revulsion, as my way was an implicit criticism of his. Accordingly his interpretations would be expressed for instance in oblique pronouncements that my penis was always in the wrong place in the wrong person at the wrong time. However, I was sufficiently compelled by a sort of conscience and a conscious need to change certain aspects of my life to remain addictively in that analysis for about one year – it was a sort of situational symbiosis that is rather different, but can be as severe as a personal symbiosis. In my second analysis with a highly politically aware analyst things were totally different. He would smile acceptingly though bemusedly at my 'polygamous' activities, and, rather than feel me disguisedly as bad and critical, by implication, of his life style, he would together with me bring about a good separateness so that we could relate to each other as loving other people. He felt that I had a 'superego' as big as a horse (I said that dinosaur might be more accurate) but it was difficult to locate the source of such an overweaning superego in my permissive and helpless parents or other family people. His comment accorded with my thinking: for want of an ordinarily produced superego I had had to invent one in a way, it so happened, that generated more and more political awareness. This way involved the internalization of all the oppressive and repressive forces in the world, so that I could be moved to at least internal tears and then action by contact with oppressed people, whereas my emotional involvement with my family of origin was infinitely less intense, especially after the age of four years when I chose to be a (non-literal) orphan and the centre of my own world. The political nature of understanding the 'superego' in this way cut across a great deal of needless psychoanalytic games-playing and the unending addictive symbiosis that such dreary games entail. It is true for many people.

Thirdly, there is addiction to work: compulsively time-regulated work with a central orientation to money-earning. For the working-class, time-regulation and money-earning are bitter, inescapable realities in capitalist society and can only gradually be changed after successful mass-revolutionary action. For the middle classes, however, conditioned consumerism and sheer (though intelligible) greed come into the picture. The central necessity for all is the achievement of *a synthesis of work with play*. This means less rigid time-regulation and facing the risk of getting less money. Parasitic middle-class occupations – in the state bureaucracy, banking, insurance, work in monopolistic companies and so on – have to be simply eliminated in the course of revolution. Non-parasitic middle-class occupations such as architecture, engineering, medicine, the arts allow generally unrealized possibilities of time destructuring-restructuring with no significant loss of productivity, though possibly less money will be earned if work increasingly becomes a form of play. This means a reduction of false needs. For instance, to quote a career that I am well acquainted with, that of the therapist, one may not after all need to own a house, car, or swimming pool, but simply floor space to sleep with another and, in the course of work, one square metre of floor space each for oneself and the other to sit on. Then warmth and simple food. Sometimes payment for therapy might be in the form of bread, fruit and so on. But addiction to work may be so severe that withdrawal results in death, hence, for example, the frequency of death from coronary thrombosis and other causes around the time of retirement. The slogan 'Never Work' is a good, provocative introduction to a re-definition of work. Its increasing adoption would help to paralyse imperializing capitalism in first-world countries. What is of more fundamental importance, however, for the future as well as the present is, as I have said, the growing coalescence of work and play. The splitting of work and play is the disastrous result of bourgeois education with its absurd binary role structures of teacher versus taught that are at an infinite remove from the original medieval university communities of Paris and Bologna. The only cure for work addiction is the transforming movement from alienated work into productive play.

To return in a very practical way to hard-drug addiction may make the general requisites for altering addictive behaviour clearer. In the most general terms what is needed is twofold. Firstly, there is the forging into existence of a will to live and to change, an action of 'forging into existence' which is the last rung of our freedom – not a capacity we were passively 'born with', nor something that can be fully intelligible in terms of what went on in our families, but an original datum of ontogenesis, an original choice, perpetually re-invented in present moments, to survive physically and as a person, a fascination with death (the wish to kill oneself more or less directly so as to avoid dying a death imposed 'from the outside') that finally has less strong a taste on the palate than the sweet savour of life. Secondly, there is needed a human context: good people whom one trusts and who do not have to act out their personal problematics against one as one withdraws from heroin, alcohol, etc. People who, in turns, can be with one every hour of the day and night with absolute constancy and maybe for many weeks with continued relationships thereafter. The choice to withdraw from one's addiction can only be made by oneself in the right context – an ordinary apartment in the community. Externally imposed and enforced withdrawal in a clinic or other medical setting invariably breaks down as soon as one is free of the external control of even 'progressive' clinic conditions. For the alcoholic* a bottle of whisky or cognac is always available but the micro-culture of the group demonstrates a clear preference for doing creative things with each other. Finally, one decides to face the pain of withdrawal and to kick the drug oneself, knowing that the group is there (and also a good physician to follow the situation and supervise medication).

What I have said about hard-drug addiction in terms

---

* 'The alcoholic' of course does not exist any more than 'the junkie' or 'the schizophrenic'. My use of these essentialistic words is nothing more than an ironic reflection on the misuse of language against people. Hard drugs like alcohol, when their use becomes addictive, may in fact, *for a time* at a certain time in one's life, be a necessary chemical destructuring that is a prelude to a radical re-structuring of one's life. But it is a perilous path, and is not to be recommended. It must be recognized, however, that an addiction may be a risky but time-delimited project during several years – *not* a career for life, though social pressures and the need for the identity of a 'junkie' or 'alcoholic', for want of any other identity, may convert a temporary voyage into a life-long exodus from life. The 'confession', 'I am an addict', may become an injunction to one's self to be that – forever; social reinforcement of this project is only too readily found.

of personal will and human context apply to all the other expressions of addiction that I have mentioned. Work with a therapist who understands these things and does not fearfully attempt to induce conformism helps make the transformation complete and, as far as the addictive patterns are concerned, final. Then other profound transformations may ensue.

Addictions essentially involve playing at Russian roulette with one's freedom. If one survives the first time it is important, to say the least, to choose to stop pulling the trigger as soon as possible. The point of stopping the addiction may be the point at which one recognizes that one has exhausted the possibility of knowing one's death through repeated 'close to death' experiences. Then stopping from the drug or pattern of behaviour becomes suddenly easy, not a tremendous struggle any more, and one can accept the agonies of the withdrawal experience. One has sufficiently and freely deterrorized one's death and one's freedom. An analogy to this is the fear of heights. This is commonly regarded as a 'neurotic symptom' but may in fact be an advance from the relatively placid 'normal' reaction to looking down at the street from a fifteenth-floor terrace. One may first cautiously stick one's head out and then crawl out onto the terrace on one's hands and knees until one is able to stand up and look down without fear. This is all about an experimentation with one's freedom, the original fear being the recognition in total lucidity that one is free to throw oneself down from the terrace, there is nothing to stop one. In this sense one has no fear of the height but only a fear of an unconditioned moment of one's freedom. The normal unafraid reaction to heights is a denial of the possibility of this encountering one's freedom in terror and then freely overcoming the fear of one's freedom. To attempt to reductively analyse this good productive fear in terms of one's gradual remembering of one's personal history is an interesting part of the process of making a life intelligible, but in relation to the issues of freedom and change it is a futile exercise. As in addiction, change does not come about through analytical insight but through an intentional alteration of one's praxis, one's way of being-acting, in the right context.

Addictions are like trying to put a badly fitting plug in the hole through which we fear our being may drain away. The irony is that what may drain away might well be something we could do without. Many addictions in fact may be security devices aimed at staying in the world or maintaining a minimally requisite contact with the normal world. Cigarettes (and alcohol and other drugs too) may be like an umbilical cord between the normal world and a self that would transcend it but fears the freedom of transcendence. The compulsive, untimely, imposed or self-imposed cessation of an addiction may be disastrous to the point of producing depression and even suicide. There is a right time, if one can find it, to stop smoking, etc. A record of heavy smoking in people with lung cancer does by no means indicate that the smoking was the *cause* of the cancer; it may well represent an attempt by the victim to *avoid* a fatal 'psychosomatic' propulsion into the cancer situation. An *advocatus diaboli* might well suggest that the lung-cancer patient dies because he did not smoke enough – smoke enough with a joyful impulse to live.

In addition to the addiction of the addict, the people immediately involved with the addict may become addicted to the addict or addicted to the addiction of the addict. Once again this involves scapegoating in the sense that those who intend to care for the addict may need him to embody their various destructive compulsivities and, should he dare get better, the others are driven away by the threat of having to take their destructiveness back into themselves. This means that, to obviate the danger of addiction to the addict, the supportive group must have strong enough centres in themselves and also a centre outside the situation of accompanying the addict through his voyage out of the inferno into a beautiful new land.

To return to etymology: if addiction is speaking *to* the other *through* something, as assigned by decree, let us revoke the decree and speak to the other only through the specific nothingness of the relationship that lies between us, never in us. This is the way to the liberating discovery of what there is to live *for*.

15

Curriculum Mortis

As I have said earlier in this book, life may be a boring distraction from death but death is certainly a boring distraction from life. However, the fact remains that the formally written out curriculum vitae for most of us has a curious irrelevance or, at the most, tangentiality to anything that we might recognize as central to our experience – however comprehensive the curriculum vitae may be – in fact the more comprehensive the worse as a rule. So a curriculum mortis, reflections on the paradoxes and delightful absurdity of usual notions of death, may prove to be more life-giving. I would like you to reflect freely on death, especially the peculiar nature of your personal death, not the anonymous, statistical deaths that most people die, and I shall present here a few of my own reflections on death to accompany yours. There are, in my experience at least, few pursuits more liberating or therapeutic in the best sense than this reflection exercise. The deep exploration of fantasies of killing oneself in different ways, the free-flowing experience of images of mutilated corpses, forms of torture, bodily putrefaction after death (particularly dead parents) constitute a therapeia that one must never allow any other person to inhibit, since this external inhibition may propel one into blind, unexperienced modes of dying.

For a long time dying in my sleep was something I feared intensely. Between the ages of four and six years my compulsive prayer before going to bed each night was 'please God, don't let me die, dream or grow old!' Apart from the obvious equation of dreaming with some sort of hypothetical post-death experience and of growing old with imminent dying, the fear of death while asleep was predominant. In fact dying in the oblivion of sleep probably never happens. Dying is so strong an experience that it will awaken us from sleep momentarily just before the moment of death arrives – it will even awaken us I believe from deep coma. The only tragic note is sounded by the fact that for so many people the only good experience of a true aloneness may happen just in this last moment.

Then there is the question of how one would like one's body to be dealt with after one's death. The Irish wake is one way – one's family and friends having a party and maybe getting drunk around one's corpse; it's a nice idea that one's dead body may be liberating too. In some countries like South Africa muslim communities in their funeral processions smile and laugh with a beautiful non-manic joy. More impressive for me was a story, of whose veracity I am not sure – but that does not seem to matter – about the way that Aldous Huxley died: he died high on acid and after his bodily death his wife read *The Tibetan Book of the Dead* next to him to accompany him in the forty-nine days between incarnations. Cremation and burial after autopsy have always seemed to me to be disrespectful not only of one's dead body but also of the history of one's body during life. What would you like to be done with your body after you die? I would like my body, as in Siberian and Mongolian Shamanistic societies, to be exposed to the elements and the birds on a bier high up on

, tree, *pace* the Public Health Authorities. Of the elements, water belongs to pre-birth, fire and earth belong to life and air is most cognate to post-death states.

It can be very difficult to distinguish between 'bad' self-depriving denial and 'good' detachment when we come to examine attitudes to death. I once attended an autopsy on one of my patients who had died of a coronary thrombosis. The pathologist, apart from doing the post-mortems, found great delight in trying, against my opposition, to stick rectal swabs up the anuses of young male schizophrenic patients' in my wards to prove a bowel toxic theory of schizophrenia. In the months before this particular autopsy he had had two major coronary attacks himself and knew the way he was going to die, but there he was carefully dissecting out the clot from the coronary artery of the cadaver. Three weeks later he had his final coronary. I think that he presented a confusion that one often encounters between alienated clinical, or other professional, non-involvement (e.g. his schizophrenia research), which is not true detachment, and a level of true detachment of which I was certain from my personal knowledge of him. The way to true dying is by treading the arduous path that leads to total detachment in the face of bodily death. In working-class cultures a sort of detachment may be achieved through a macabre but down-to-earth humour.

In the act of killing oneself* one may discover new ways of achieving detachment. It is a commonplace to assert that killing oneself has an aggressive intent towards others who are closely involved with oneself. I believe this to be untrue in the last critical moment of life, since

* The use of the word suicide, a translation of the act of killing oneself into Latin, is a euphemistic attempt to make the reality of the act less real. It's very much like calling black people negroes.

the choice to die is sufficiently immense to erase all lesser sentiments, even the most powerful angry feelings. So for others to feel aggressed against simply misses the point. Also guilt is the supreme bourgeois indulgence, the ultimate family vice. All guilt is aggression against its object. Society is so threatened by people who kill themselves (in terms of the obvious implication that none of its rules and organization really matter, 'suicide' is a standing invitation to anomie) that attempts to kill oneself are still regarded as criminal offences in many countries. In early nineteenth-century England it was regarded as a capital offence - one should be legally murdered for daring to try to kill oneself. For example, one man tried unsuccessfully to kill himself by cutting his throat and was sentenced to death by hanging – but before the hanging (in those days slow strangulation rather than death by rapid trauma to the central nervous system) his wound had to be carefully stitched up and bandaged so that it would not open and allow him to bleed to death from a self-inflicted wound. He could only die by the legally prescribed form of hanging.

There is in psychiatry a very precise analogue to this historical absurdity. One of the most malign forms of psychiatric and psychotherapeutic interference in the life of the victim ('patient') is determined by the fear-ridden determination of the psychiatrist to stop the victim trying to kill himself, since if the latter does this the 'treatment' will be seen by others as 'bad'. This fear deforms to a major extent much of what goes on in psychiatric institutions. 'Good treatment' stops the victim killing himself and replaces the possibility of this act by a 'legally', i.e. medically and professionally, correct form of murder – a properly prescribed death for the victim by The Cure, the successful outcome of treatment in which the victim gasps out 'thank you' with the last breath of his life before returning to the Golgotha of The Normal Life to which he has been led finally to submit. He feels more or less vaguely the sacrificial pain of the loss of all that was familiar and might have been loved in himself to the broken shell of a conformist non-self. It would be a condign retribution to his psychiatrist to realize that *he* exists in just such a condition himself and that all he was concerned about was not to share in an experience of the truth of the other person with the other, but simply to arrange for his victim to confirm his, the psychiatrist's, correctness in therapeutic practice. The doctor, thoroughly trained to blind himself to any glimmer of a liberatory hope for himself, contents himself with an absence, the insides of an empty but expectant coffin, with his infinitely comfortable and unspeakably hideous state of unshakable non-guilt.

For some people the only path to ecstatic experience they discover, despite the fact that there are many others such as political and religious ecstasy, psychedelic substances, epilepsy, meditation and so on, is by killing themselves in certain ways. For instance, I knew a man who jumped from near the top of the very high Post Office Tower in London, after calculating that it would take him about ten seconds to reach the bottom – ten seconds of experience that would exceed in intensity all the experience in his previous life. In fact he ecstatically flew over ten yards from the base of the tower.

I believe that killing oneself is always a mistaken path to transcendence, but the right to kill oneself must be absolute – despite the absurdities of bourgeois law, Life Insurance companies and so on. This is a sister situation to entering revolutionary areas of action where one is likely to be killed. That is not only a right but now it is an imperative. We live in times in which total risk has become necessary.

*

Certain passages in this book and my previous writings refer more or less directly to reincarnation, especially when I write of post-death experience. Perhaps then it is time for me to throw some beam of light, however slender, on what I understand by this term. Obviously one cannot believe in crude thinking to the effect that after one's death the person, mind, spirit that one has been enters the bodily existence of a new person or animal – the 'higher' one's reincarnation form being determined by the merits one has accrued in one's previous life. What seems to me to be the case, after searching through the remotest regions of my experience, is that when we die biologically we cease to be us as persons in any sense but remain regeneratively in the cosmos if we understand cosmos as 'all that is' – beyond the reaches of scientific cosmology. The I that is no longer me resides in spaces that are not places, specific locations that are anywhere and everywhere, but in such a way that the *specificity* is not lost – the specificity is the 'incarnation'. If all this seems to be paradoxical, it is simply because language was devised to deal technically with material things, with social relations and with the expression of beauty – never with the realm of experience with which we are concerned here. The cyclical *sequences* of death and rebirth are illusion except in the sense of movements between being in our minds and being out of them during our present corporeal life-span.

I use the word specificity as a sign that after personal death *there is experiencing* in which the 'I' is absorbed, *but there is no 'I' to do the experiencing*. We begin to get the feel of this by traversing any of a number of paths that lead to a magnified awareness: mystical experience, the correct use of 'psychedelic' substances* including autonomously generated, chemical change in illness (often in the immediate post-epileptic state, in advanced pulmonary tuberculosis and so on) and in health under certain conditions; this points clearly to the need to develop a phenomenological chemistry that, amongst other things, would involve a re-examination of alchemy. The other path that I have tried to begin to trace out in the segment or chapter entitled 'The Transpositions of Meditation' is of course meditation which may bring the most truly autonomous chemical changes.

So post-death experience, 'belonging' to no one, is located in the cosmos understood as the being of 'all that is' but there is also the being in the mode of 'the all that is not'. Nothing *is* in the sense that there is a phenomenology of Nothing that is concerned with experiencing all around the perimeter of Nothing. This perimetric experiencing points towards the Nothing and renders it specific, but 'within' the Nothing there is no experiencing. Crossing the perimeter is the step beyond transpersonal post-death experiencing and is the final mergence with the Clear Light of the Void. Whatever credence one chooses to place in the phenomenology of post-death experiencing as related in *The Tibetan Book of the Dead*, one thing is certain: *the Void is that which is finally beyond the ultimate moment of experience*. It is where experience finally points but cannot cross the threshold.

*

* Including 'ordinary' foods such as massive quantities of garlic, some eastern combinations of spices, and opium when consumed as a foodstuff in the Orient in a way that does not become addictive in certain cultures.

This section is continuous with 'Experience to the Guillotine' so I shall depart from the examination of death in direct terms and, in the form of *obiter dicta*, explore some related modes of deadly mutilation of experience.

Bourgeois welfare is farewell, a farewell said (or left unsaid) by the welfare worker to her/his clients. But there is urban guerrilla warfare and also urban guerrilla welfare and that is different. The guerrilla achieves a solidarity with the people that aims not only at their future liberation but at a very present accompaniment for them in their very present travail. Guerrillas fight with the people as lawyers, doctors, guardians of the people's courts and people's prisons, and so on. This form of welfare does not exclude from its ambit police and militia whose indoctrinated paranoia we recognize – though in the course of armed insurrection, the last and decisive resort, we may inexorably have to shoot some of them in generous acts of counter-violence. It's all part of the curriculum mortis.

*

The Weberian charisma needs re-definition. Charisma (from Greek χάρις – favour) is nothing less than its diffusion from the appointed and self-appointed charismatic leader to the masses of people. The charisma of the charismatic leader is the conjoint creation of the masses and the leader who is part of the masses. So the true guru discovers the guru-nature not in himself but in the masses of which he is a part. Otherwise all die according to an authoritarian prescription for death.

*

The middle-class radicals waste years arguing about the relation of supra-structure to infra-structure. One may accept the classical definitions but not sacrifice the vision of what underlies the infra-structure nor relegate it to just another aspect of the supra-structural. What underlies and may undercut both levels is all of our elected freedoms. These freedoms are a nothing but a specific, active nothing and *that* is really something. In terror we regard the nothingness of our freedoms as some sort of death. All I can say is that in such a case, if we follow our terror to the limit, this sort of death is the only death worth dying.

*

Next the Obscene and a judgement on the cadaveric judges of the obscene. Etymologically obscenity refers to augury, divination of the future by observing the nature and trajectory of the flight of birds. In short bird-watching. All the most decent judges, official and unofficial, censors and clerics are secretly addicted to bird-watching. So too with pornography – the description of the manners of harlots; the final describers of these phenomena are the very respectable judges themselves but they are conditioned to convert their own delight in talented pornography into prohibition for everyone else. The Spanish phrase *Prohibido prohibir* must now reign supreme.

We shall combat the blind enemy not only by ballistic assault but also by assaults against hegemonic male chauvinism, normal and normally infrequent, non-orgasmic, heterosexual, penis-vagina marital rape, and edadism – restrictions of sex-love on grounds of age. Small children, as has been clearly demonstrated, can have orgasm too and the sooner initiation is achieved the better; also female and male menopause must not lead to anything but an intensification of orgasmic experience – not an attitude of weary resignation that one 'does not have to do it any more'. Female primates of other species remain fertile until they are too old to move. A man aged eighty-two once told me that making love after the age of eighty was less frequent but much better. In the curriculum mortis we find that all excuses for non-sexuality in any form are nothing but brief obituaries.

The judges of the obscene would establish 'Soul Servicing Stations' and an obligatory 'Ministry of Social Sanity Test', perhaps every two years, so that people may or may not retain their licence for non-love, non-sex, imbecilic normalcy and metaphorical death throughout the span of all of their unlived lives.

*

Finally, our curriculum runs on until we arrive at that lethal mutilation of experience called aesthetics. No concept of beauty is viable now. Beauty is dead and aesthetics must return to its original sense of feeling with (and beyond) all our senses. We have passed the last day of 'great' one-name works of art and have entered the time of communal creation. Henceforth there will be no more Beethovens, no more Rembrandts, no more Tolstoys. Their works will endure all the vicissitudes of time to come but in the time to come the manifestations of the beautiful, transformed then into revolutionary *truth*, will be the productions of all of us. This is the only way out of a dead and deadening aesthetics. We shall create a quotidian Dada, an anti-aesthetics of everyday life. What is beyond the beautiful will be invented by the revolutionary act, created by subtle gestures, your eyes meeting mine in the street and our seeing each other for the first time, a vision of a Chinese girl bending to tie her shoe laces with the tips of her long black hair caressing the pavement, and it will be created by the discovery of the unordered discipline or our true madness.

The guillotine of experience crumbles after the sufficient work of the worms of revolution.

The curriculum mortis shall finally run out.

My next book will be different.

It will not be by me.